OPPOSING
VIEWPOINTS®
SERIES

D0446847

Tobacco and Smoking

Other Books of Related Interest:

Opposing Viewpoints Series

Gateway Drugs

Teen Drug Abuse

Current Controversies

Smoking

At Issue Series

Teen Smoking

"Congress shall make
no law . . . abridging
the freedom of speech,
or of the press."

First Amendment to the U.S. Constitution

The basic foundation of our democracy is the First Amendment guarantee of freedom of expression. The *Opposing Viewpoints* Series is dedicated to the concept of this basic freedom and the idea that it is more important to practice it than to enshrine it.

Tobacco and Smoking

Susan Hunnicutt, Book Editor

GREENHAVEN PRESS
A part of Gale, Cengage Learning

Detroit • New York • San Francisco • New Haven, Conn • Waterville, Maine • London

GALE
CENGAGE Learning

Christine Nasso, *Publisher*
Elizabeth Des Chenes, *Managing Editor*

© 2009 Greenhaven Press, a part of Gale, Cengage Learning

Gale and Greenhaven Press are registered trademarks used herein under license.

For more information, contact:
Greenhaven Press
27500 Drake Rd.
Farmington Hills, MI 48331-3535
Or you can visit our Internet site at gale.cengage.com

For product information and technology assistance, contact us at

Gale Customer Support, 1-800-877-4253
For permission to use material from this text or product, submit all requests online at
www.cengage.com/permissions

Further permissions questions can be emailed to permissionrequest@cengage.com

Articles in Greenhaven Press anthologies are often edited for length to meet page requirements. In addition, original titles of these works are changed to clearly present the main thesis and to explicitly indicate the author's opinion. Every effort is made to ensure that Greenhaven Press accurately reflects the original intent of the authors. Every effort has been made to trace the owners of copyrighted material.

Cover image © Taxi/Getty Images

LIBRARY OF CONGRESS CATALOGING-IN-PUBLICATION DATA

Tobacco and smoking / Susan Hunnicutt, book editor.
    p. cm. -- (Opposing viewpoints)
  Includes bibliographical references and index.
  ISBN 978-0-7377-4242-8 (hardcover)
  ISBN 978-0-7377-4243-5 (pbk.)
  1. Tobacco use--United States. 2. Smoking--United States. 3. Tobacco industry--United States. I. Hunnicutt, Susan.
  HV5760.T62 2009
  362.29'620973--dc22
                                                          2008028546

Printed in the United States of America
1 2 3 4 5 6 7 12 11 10 09 08

Contents

Why Consider Opposing Viewpoints?   11

Introduction   14

Chapter 1: Is Tobacco Use a Serious Problem?

Chapter Preface   20

1. Smoking Is Harmful to Human Health   23
   National Institute on Drug Abuse

2. The Dangers of Smoking Are Exaggerated   30
   Paul Johnson

3. Secondhand Smoke Is a Serious Problem   36
   Richard Carmona

4. The Dangers of Secondhand Smoke   44
   Are Exaggerated
   Jacob Sullum

5. Smokeless Tobacco Is Harmful to   49
   Human Health
   Business Wire

6. Smokeless Tobacco Is Less Harmful to   54
   Human Health Than Smoking
   Brad Rodu and William T. Godshall

7. Efforts to Reduce Teen Smoking Have Stalled   61
   William V. Corr

8. Teen Smoking Rates Have Declined   67
   Dave Gershman

Periodical Bibliography   72

Chapter 2: How Can Tobacco Use Be Reduced?

Chapter Preface   **74**

1. Governments Should Tax Tobacco to Save Lives   **76**
   Prabhat Jha

2. The Government Should Not Tax Tobacco   **81**
   A.O. Kime

3. Most Americans Believe Smoking Should Be Banned in Public Places   **90**
   Stephen Kaufman

4. Smoking Should Not Be Banned in Public Places   **95**
   Joseph Bast

5. Smoking Prevention Efforts Should Focus on Children   **101**
   Leann M. Lesperance and Henry H. Bernstein

6. It Could Be a Mistake to Focus Smoking Prevention Efforts on Children   **106**
   Ronald Bayer and Valeri Kiesig

Periodical Bibliography   **112**

Chapter 3: Should the Food and Drug Administration Regulate Tobacco?

Chapter Preface   **114**

1. The Food and Drug Administration Should Have the Authority to Regulate Tobacco Products   **117**
   Edward M. Kennedy

2. The Food and Drug Administration Should Not Be Responsible for Regulating Tobacco   **126**
   Andrew C. von Eschenbach

3. FDA Regulation Would Protect Tobacco Companies from the Threat of Litigation   **135**
   Michael Siegel

4. FDA Regulation of Tobacco Would Unfairly   141
   Benefit the Largest Tobacco Companies
   Joseph A. Rotondi

5. The FDA Tobacco Bill Is a Misguided   149
   Piece of Legislation
   Forces International

Periodical Bibliography   159

Chapter 4: How Do the Media Impact Individuals' Choices to Smoke or Not Smoke?

Chapter Preface   161

1. Tobacco Advertising Is Harmful to Public Health   163
   Physicians for a Smoke-Free Canada

2. Tobacco Advertising Does Not Directly   176
   Cause People to Smoke
   Jacob Sullum

3. The Tobacco Industry's Smoking Prevention Ads   187
   Increase the Likelihood That Teens Will Smoke
   American Legacy Foundation

4. Smoking Behavior Should Not Be Censored   192
   in the Movies
   Evan R. Goldstein

5. Images of Smoking in the Media Encourage   196
   Youth to Smoke
   Tara Parker-Pope

Periodical Bibliography   201

For Further Discussion   202

Organizations to Contact   205

Bibliography of Books   210

Index   213

Why Consider Opposing Viewpoints?

> *"The only way in which a human being can make some approach to knowing the whole of a subject is by hearing what can be said about it by persons of every variety of opinion and studying all modes in which it can be looked at by every character of mind. No wise man ever acquired his wisdom in any mode but this."*
>
> *John Stuart Mill*

In our media-intensive culture it is not difficult to find differing opinions. Thousands of newspapers and magazines and dozens of radio and television talk shows resound with differing points of view. The difficulty lies in deciding which opinion to agree with and which "experts" seem the most credible. The more inundated we become with differing opinions and claims, the more essential it is to hone critical reading and thinking skills to evaluate these ideas. *Opposing Viewpoints* books address this problem directly by presenting stimulating debates that can be used to enhance and teach these skills. The varied opinions contained in each book examine many different aspects of a single issue. While examining these conveniently edited opposing views, readers can develop critical thinking skills such as the ability to compare and contrast authors' credibility, facts, argumentation styles, use of persuasive techniques, and other stylistic tools. In short, the *Opposing Viewpoints* series is an ideal way to attain the higher-level thinking and reading skills so essential in a culture of diverse and contradictory opinions.

In addition to providing a tool for critical thinking, *Opposing Viewpoints* books challenge readers to question their own strongly held opinions and assumptions. Most people form their opinions on the basis of upbringing, peer pressure, and personal, cultural, or professional bias. By reading carefully balanced opposing views, readers must directly confront new ideas as well as the opinions of those with whom they disagree. This is not to simplistically argue that everyone who reads opposing views will—or should—change his or her opinion. Instead, the series enhances readers' understanding of their own views by encouraging confrontation with opposing ideas. Careful examination of others' views can lead to the readers' understanding of the logical inconsistencies in their own opinions, perspective on why they hold an opinion, and the consideration of the possibility that their opinion requires further evaluation.

Evaluating Other Opinions

To ensure that this type of examination occurs, *Opposing Viewpoints* books present all types of opinions. Prominent spokespeople on different sides of each issue as well as well-known professionals from many disciplines challenge the reader. An additional goal of the series is to provide a forum for other, less known, or even unpopular viewpoints. The opinion of an ordinary person who has had to make the decision to cut off life support from a terminally ill relative, for example, may be just as valuable and provide just as much insight as a medical ethicist's professional opinion. The editors have two additional purposes in including these less known views. One, the editors encourage readers to respect others' opinions—even when not enhanced by professional credibility. It is only by reading or listening to and objectively evaluating others' ideas that one can determine whether they are worthy of consideration. Two, the inclusion of such viewpoints encourages the important critical thinking skill of objectively evaluating an author's credentials and bias. This evaluation will illuminate an author's reasons for taking a particular stance on an issue and will aid in readers' evaluation of the author's ideas.

It is our hope that these books will give readers a deeper understanding of the issues debated and an appreciation of the complexity of even seemingly simple issues when good and honest people disagree. This awareness is particularly important in a democratic society such as ours in which people enter into public debate to determine the common good. Those with whom one disagrees should not be regarded as enemies but rather as people whose views deserve careful examination and may shed light on one's own.

Thomas Jefferson once said that "difference of opinion leads to inquiry, and inquiry to truth." Jefferson, a broadly educated man, argued that "if a nation expects to be ignorant and free. . .it expects what never was and never will be." As individuals and as a nation, it is imperative that we consider the opinions of others and examine them with skill and discernment. The *Opposing Viewpoints* series is intended to help readers achieve this goal.

David L. Bender and Bruno Leone,
Founders

Introduction

"Since 1613, when John Rolfe introduced a successful experiment in tobacco cultivation in Virginia, the leaf has assumed major social, industrial, economic and medical implications. Consequently, persons concerned with tobacco on a commercial or personal basis have been subject to a variety of different regulations over the past 360 years. . . . The motivation for regulation has come from both sides of the controversy." —History of Tobacco Regulation, Schaffer Library of Drug Policy

On November 23, 1998, forty-six states, as well as American Samoa, the District of Columbia, Guam, Puerto Rico, the Northern Mariana Islands, and the U.S. Virgin Islands, entered into a binding legal agreement with the largest manufacturers of tobacco in the United States. In addition to payments to the states of more than $206 billion over twenty-five years, making it the largest civil settlement in United States history, tobacco manufacturers agreed to significant limitations on their advertising and marketing activities, and a range of other restrictive and prescriptive measures aimed at reducing youth access to, and consumption of, cigarettes. In return for these concessions, the agreement exempted the tobacco companies from liability in the future for medical expenses incurred by the states as the result of tobacco-related illnesses. It settled all pending consumer protection and antitrust lawsuits, releasing tobacco manufacturers from liability for "past, present and certain future claims against them."

The Tobacco Master Settlement Agreement (MSA), as it was called, came about because of a proven relationship between the use of tobacco products and a number of common and serious health conditions, including heart disease, lung cancer, and emphysema. This is explicitly stated in the so-called Model Statute, part of the agreement which outlines legislative actions that may be taken by individual states that are parties to the MSA: "The Surgeon General has determined that smoking causes lung cancer, heart disease and other serious diseases, and that there are hundreds of thousands of tobacco-related deaths in the United States each year." The MSA was implemented in part to coordinate the legal claims of the states against the tobacco industry, shifting the financial burden for tobacco-related health care costs from the states to the tobacco manufacturers in a systematic and orderly way. Prior to the MSA's drafting, four states—Florida, Minnesota, Mississippi, and Texas—had already mounted successful legal actions against the tobacco industry to recover tobacco-related health care expenses, and had settled with the tobacco manufacturers for $40 billion, and legal actions were pending in several other states.

In addition to monetary payments that would be made by the tobacco companies to the forty-six states that were party to the agreement, and restrictions on advertising and marketing of tobacco products, the MSA established the American Legacy Foundation, an advocacy organization that produces media campaigns aimed at educating young people about the health risks and dangers of tobacco use. Although no rigid guidelines or requirements exist, states participating in the MSA are also expected to use proceeds of the agreement to fund tobacco prevention and tobacco cessation programs.

Criticism of the MSA has come from many quarters. For example attorney Thomas C. O'Brien, in a policy brief for the Cato Institute (a libertarian think tank that advocates for the principles of limited government, individual liberty, and free markets), alleged early on that the Tobacco Master Settlement Agreement was illegal and unconstitutional, and that the protections from liability awarded to the tobacco manufacturers amounted to a blank check for monopolists. The MSA is "a sophisticated, white-collar crime instigated by contingency-fee lawyers in pursuit of unimaginable riches," O'Brien wrote. "In collaboration with state attorneys general and the four leading tobacco companies, they concocted a scheme that forces all tobacco companies—even new companies and companies that didn't join the settlement—to engage in a program of price fixing and monopolization. Essentially, the major cigarette makers bought permission to fix prices and exclude competitors."

According to O'Brien's analysis, the presumed beneficiaries of the agreement—smokers who have become ill as a result of the use of tobacco—are actually the MSA's inadvertent victims. They "get nothing out of the settlement yet must pay the entire cost" through increases in the cost of cigarettes. Because the states are receiving billions of dollars as a result of the agreement, O'Brien suggested it is unlikely that states' attorneys general will prosecute tobacco companies for violations of existing antitrust laws.

Surprisingly, the MSA attracted similar criticism from anti-smoking advocates. In a speech at the National Tobacco Control Conference in 1999, William Godshall, founder and executive director of Smokefree Pennsylvania, argued that the MSA provided "far greater benefits for tobacco manufacturers than for public health," and that tobacco companies actually became more powerful as a result of the agreement. Godshall accused the states' attorneys general of overstating the benefits of the agreement while failing to acknowledge that it actually shields tobacco manufacturers from future liability for injuries or medical costs associated with the use of tobacco.

Since 1998, four organizations—the American Heart Association, the American Cancer Society, Campaign for Tobacco-

Free Kids, and the American Lung Association—have cooperated to produce yearly reports assessing the states' use of MSA funds. The 2007 report, *A Broken Promise to Our Children: The 1998 State Tobacco Settlement Nine Years Later*, found that in spite of recent increases in funding for tobacco prevention and cessation programs, most states still do not support such programs at the minimum levels recommended by the Centers for Disease Control and Prevention. "If the nation is to continue reducing smoking and other tobacco use, Congress and the states must resist complacency and redouble efforts to implement proven tobacco control measures," the report stated. "These include fully-funded tobacco prevention programs, higher tobacco taxes and smoke-free workplace laws at the state level and U.S. Food and Drug Administration (FDA) regulation of tobacco products, higher tobacco taxes and a national public education campaign at the federal level."

The findings of *A Broken Promise to Our Children* echo those of a 2005 paper published in the journal *Health Affairs*. That study found that state allocation of MSA funds has frequently not been in line with the stated goals of the lawsuits that led up to the settlements. The failure of the states to enact tobacco control measures envisioned in the MSA reflect "a lack of strong advocacy from public health interest groups, an unreliable public constituency for tobacco control, and inconsistent support from state executive and legislative branches, all combined with sizable budget deficits that provided competing uses for settlement funds."

The Tobacco Master Settlement Agreement has attracted intense criticism from a variety of interested parties. The adversarial tone of the conversation around the MSA resembles that of other debates covered in this book: Is Tobacco Use a Serious Problem? How Can Tobacco Use Be Reduced? Should the Food and Drug Administration Regulate Tobacco? and How Do the Media Impact Individuals' Choices to Smoke or Not Smoke? While covering a wide range of issues, they all reflect on the central question of how society should respond to what is known about the specific ways tobacco use endangers human health.

OPPOSING
VIEWPOINTS®
SERIES

CHAPTER 1

Is Tobacco Use a Serious Problem?

Chapter Preface

When European explorers arrived on the American continents in the late fifteenth century, the use of tobacco by Native Americans was among the earliest of their discoveries. Soon after Columbus arrived on the island that is now Cuba, he observed tobacco being smoked in "sticks," and when he returned to Europe, tobacco leaves and seeds were among the items he carried. Later, through many encounters, it was learned that tobacco played a central role in myths of origin as well as the practices of many Native American peoples. It was used to create bonds among tribal groups, in ceremonies marking the beginnings of new undertakings, and to procure blessings from the spirit world.

In 1612, settlers of Jamestown, Virginia, were the first Europeans to grow tobacco for commercial purposes. Slaves from Africa harvested Jamestown tobacco and, very soon, it became one of the most important exports and an essential commodity contributing to the success of the colonies. A robust tobacco industry was a main source of funding for the American Revolution. Thus, from the earliest days, tobacco has been an important part of the story of the Americas.

The use of tobacco by Europeans was controversial, however, from the very beginning. King James I of England found it to be "lothsome to the eye, hatefull to the Nosse, harmefull to the braine, dangerous to the Lungs, and in the blacke stinking fume thereof, nearest resembling the horrible Stigian smoke of the pit that is bottomelesse." He published a broadside—as public notices were called—attacking the use of tobacco, and laws were passed imposing heavy tariffs on tobacco imports. Despite these restrictions, however, growth of the tobacco trade was rapid, both in Europe and in the colonies. Tobacco was smoked in pipes, chewed, or used as snuff. By the late 1860s, cigarettes had become a popular tobacco delivery system, while one American observer reported that the use of chewing tobacco was almost universal.

It was not until the 1930s that literature addressing the dangers of tobacco use began to appear. European scientists reported a statistical correlation between smoking and cancer, and a few years later, researchers at Johns Hopkins University observed that smokers had shorter lives. In 1944, even before a causal relationship between tobacco use and cancer could be proven, the American Cancer Society began to publish warnings about the possible dangers of smoking.

In the 1950s, the tobacco interests responded to scientific studies of the health effects of tobacco use by forming the Tobacco Industry Research Council (TIRC). Following the advice of TIRC, manufacturers began to produce filtered cigarettes and lower-tar cigarettes, purportedly "healthier" products, which were designed to assuage the public's fears.

Evidence of the ill health effects of tobacco use continued to accumulate, however. When the first report of the Surgeon General's Advisory Committee on Smoking and Health was released in 1964, it was based on more than 7,000 biomedical research articles that showed a definitive relationship between smoking, lung cancer, and laryngeal cancer in men, and which identified smoking as a major cause of chronic bronchitis. While research had not yet proven that smoking caused lung cancer in women, a sizable body of evidence showed that this was probably also true. The Surgeon General's report was among the most influential news stories of 1964.

In 1965, the U.S. Congress passed the Federal Cigarette Labeling and Advertising Act, which required a health warning on cigarette packages and banned cigarette advertising in the broadcast media. The Public Health Service established the National Clearinghouse for Smoking and Health, later replaced by the Centers for Disease Control and Prevention's Office on Smoking and Health. Since that time, the U.S. government has provided support for a variety of initiatives designed to educate the public about the health dangers of tobacco and to reduce its use. In spite of the preponderance of evidence linking tobacco to cancer and also to heart disease, 45 million Americans still smoke, and millions use other forms of tobacco products that have known health risks.

Given these facts, should tobacco use be considered a serious problem? Today, the forms of this question have multiplied, even as they have become more nuanced. Is tobacco use so serious a problem that the government should limit the choices available to adults, or is smoking essentially a civil liberties issue? Is secondhand or environmental smoke dangerous enough to enact statutes outlawing smoking in public places? What about the relative dangers of new, ostensibly safer products that continue to be developed by the tobacco industry?

These are some of questions that are addressed in this chapter.

> *"The cigarette is a very efficient and highly engineered drug delivery system. By inhaling tobacco smoke, the average smoker takes in 1 to 2 mg of nicotine per cigarette."*

Smoking Is Harmful to Human Health

National Institute on Drug Abuse

In the following viewpoint, the National Institute on Drug Abuse (NIDA) argues that although the use of tobacco has declined, 70.3 million Americans over the age of twelve continue to use tobacco. NIDA believes tobacco products are drug delivery systems, and the drug they deliver—nicotine—is highly addictive. Furthermore, NIDA claims, tobacco use remains the leading preventable cause of death in the United States, with cigarette smoking killing an estimated 440,000 U.S. citizens each year— more than alcohol, cocaine, heroin, homicide, suicide, car accidents, fire, and AIDS combined. NIDA also points out that cigarette smoking harms every organ in the body, and is responsible for approximately one-third of all cancer deaths. The National Institute on Drug Abuse is a federal scientific research institute under the National Institutes of Health.

National Institute on Drug Abuse, *Tobacco Addiction* (Research Report Series), NIH Publication No. 06-4342, 2006. www.nida.nih.gov. Reproduced by permission.

As you read, consider the following questions:

1. How many chemicals can be found in tobacco smoke?

2. What causes the "kick" that many smokers experience?

3. What are some of the withdrawal symptoms experienced by smokers?

According to the 2004 National Survey on Drug Use and Health, an estimated 70.3 million Americans age 12 or older reported current use of tobacco—59.9 million (24.9 percent of the population) were current cigarette smokers, 13.7 million (5.7 percent) smoked cigars, 1.8 million (0.8 percent) smoked pipes, and 7.2 million (3.0 percent) used smokeless tobacco, confirming that tobacco is one of the most widely abused substances in the United States. While these numbers are still unacceptably high, they represent a decrease of almost 50 percent since peak use in 1965.

NIDA's [National Institute on Drug Abuse] 2005 Monitoring the Future Survey of 8th-, 10th-, and 12th-graders, used to track drug use patterns and attitudes, has also shown a striking decrease in smoking trends among the Nation's youth. The latest results indicate that about 9 percent of 8th-graders, 15 percent of 10th-graders, and 23 percent of 12th-graders had used cigarettes in the 30 days prior to the survey. Despite cigarette use being at the lowest levels of the survey since a peak in the mid-1990s, the past few years indicate a clear slowing of this decline. And while perceived risk and disapproval of smoking had been on the rise, recent years have shown the rate of change to be dwindling. In fact, current use, perceived risk, and disapproval leveled off among 8th-graders in 2005, suggesting that renewed efforts are needed to ensure that teens understand the harmful consequences of smoking.

Moreover, the declining prevalence of cigarette smoking among the general U.S. population is not reflected in patients with mental illnesses. For them, it remains substantially higher, with the incidence of smoking in patients suffering from posttraumatic stress disorder, bipolar disorder, major depression, and other mental illness twofold to fourfold higher than the general population, and smoking incidence among people with schizophrenia as high as 90 percent.

Tobacco use is the leading preventable cause of death in the United States. The impact of tobacco use in terms of morbidity [illness] and mortality costs to society is staggering. Economically, more than $75 billion of total U.S. healthcare costs each year is attributable directly to smoking. However, this cost is well below the total cost to society because it does not include burn care from smoking-related fires, perinatal care for low birth-weight infants of mothers who smoke, and medical care costs associated with disease caused by second-hand smoke. In addition to healthcare costs, the costs of lost productivity due to smoking effects are estimated at $82 billion per year, bringing a conservative estimate of the economic burden of smoking to more than $150 billion per year.

How Does Tobacco Deliver Its Effects?

There are more than 4,000 chemicals found in the smoke of tobacco products. Of these, nicotine, first identified in the early 1800s, is the primary reinforcing component of tobacco that acts on the brain.

Cigarette smoking is the most popular method of using tobacco; however, there has also been a recent increase in the sale and consumption of smokeless tobacco products, such as snuff and chewing tobacco. These smokeless products also contain nicotine, as well as many toxic chemicals.

The cigarette is a very efficient and highly engineered drug delivery system. By inhaling tobacco smoke, the average smoker takes in 1 to 2 mg of nicotine per cigarette. When tobacco is smoked, nicotine rapidly reaches peak levels in the bloodstream and enters the brain. A typical smoker will take 10 puffs on a cigarette over a period of 5 minutes that the cigarette is lit. Thus, a person who smokes about [1.5] packs

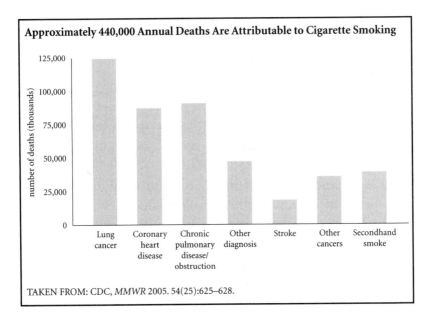

Approximately 440,000 Annual Deaths Are Attributable to Cigarette Smoking

TAKEN FROM: CDC, *MMWR* 2005. 54(25):625–628.

(30 cigarettes) daily gets 300 "hits" of nicotine to the brain each day. In those who typically do not inhale the smoke—such as cigar and pipe smokers and smokeless tobacco users—nicotine is absorbed through the mucosal membranes and reaches peak blood levels and the brain more slowly.

Immediately after exposure to nicotine, there is a "kick" caused in part by the drug's stimulation of the adrenal glands and resulting discharge of epinephrine (adrenaline). The rush of adrenaline stimulates the body and causes a sudden release of glucose, as well as an increase in blood pressure, respiration, and heart rate. Nicotine also suppresses insulin output from the pancreas, which means that smokers are always slightly hyperglycemic (i.e., they have elevated blood sugar levels). The calming effect of nicotine reported by many users is usually associated with a decline in withdrawal effects rather than direct effects of nicotine.

Is Nicotine Addictive?

Yes. Most smokers use tobacco regularly because they are addicted to nicotine. Addiction is characterized by compulsive drug seeking and use, even in the face of negative health consequences. It is well documented that most smokers identify tobacco use as harmful and express a desire to reduce or stop using it, and nearly 35 million of them want to quit each year. Unfortunately, only about 6 percent of people who try to quit are successful for more than a month.

Research has shown how nicotine acts on the brain to produce a number of effects. Of primary importance to its addictive nature are findings that nicotine activates reward pathways—the brain circuitry that regulates feelings of pleasure. A key brain chemical involved in mediating the desire to consume drugs is the neurotransmitter dopamine, and research has shown that nicotine increases levels of dopamine in the reward circuits. This reaction is similar to that seen with other drugs of abuse, and is thought to underlie the pleasurable sensations experienced by many smokers. Nicotine's pharmacokinetic properties [i.e., how a drug is absorbed and metabolized] also enhance its abuse potential. Cigarette smoking produces a rapid distribution of nicotine to the brain, with drug levels peaking within 10 seconds of inhalation. However, the acute effects of nicotine dissipate in a few minutes, as do the associated feelings of reward, which causes the smoker to continue dosing to maintain the drug's pleasurable effects and prevent withdrawal.

Nicotine withdrawal symptoms include irritability, craving, cognitive and attentional deficits, sleep disturbances, and increased appetite. These symptoms may begin within a few hours after the last cigarette, quickly driving people back to tobacco use. Symptoms peak within the first few days of smoking cessation and may subside within a few weeks. For some people, however, symptoms may persist for months.

While withdrawal is related to the pharmacological effects of nicotine, many behavioral factors can also affect the severity of withdrawal symptoms. For some people, the feel, smell, and sight of a cigarette and the ritual of obtaining, handling, lighting, and smoking the cigarette are all associated with the pleasurable effects of smoking and can make withdrawal or craving worse. While nicotine gum and patches may alleviate the pharmacological aspects of withdrawal, cravings often persist. Other forms of nicotine replacement, such as inhalers, attempt to address some of these other issues, while behavioral therapies can help smokers identify environmental triggers of withdrawal and craving so they can employ strategies to prevent or circumvent these symptoms and urges. . . .

What Are the Medical Consequences of Tobacco Use?

Cigarette smoking kills an estimated 440,000 U.S. citizens each year—more than alcohol, cocaine, heroin, homicide, suicide, car accidents, fire, and AIDS combined. Since 1964, more than 12 million Americans have died prematurely from smoking, and another 25 million U.S. smokers alive today will most likely die of a smoking-related illness.

Cigarette smoking harms every organ in the body. It has been conclusively linked to leukemia, cataracts, and pneumonia, and accounts for about one-third of all cancer deaths. The overall rates of death from cancer are twice as high among smokers as nonsmokers, with heavy smokers having rates that are four times greater than those of nonsmokers. Foremost among the cancers caused by tobacco use is lung cancer— cigarette smoking has been linked to about 90 percent of all lung cancer cases, the number-one cancer killer of both men and women. Smoking is also associated with cancers of the mouth, pharynx, larynx, esophagus, stomach, pancreas, cervix, kidney, ureter, and bladder.

In addition to cancer, smoking causes lung diseases such as chronic bronchitis and emphysema, and it has been found to exacerbate asthma symptoms in adults and children. More than 90 percent of all deaths from chronic obstructive pulmonary diseases are attributable to cigarette smoking. It has also been well documented that smoking substantially increases the risk of heart disease, including stroke, heart attack, vascular disease, and aneurysm. It is estimated that smoking accounts for approximately 21 percent of deaths from coronary heart disease each year.

Exposure to high doses of nicotine, such as those found in some insecticide sprays, can be extremely toxic as well, causing vomiting, tremors, convulsions, and death. In fact, one drop of pure nicotine can kill a person. Nicotine poisoning has been reported from accidental ingestion of insecticides by adults and ingestion of tobacco products by children and pets. Death usually results in a few minutes from respiratory failure caused by paralysis.

While we often think of medical consequences that result from direct use of tobacco products, passive or secondary smoke also increases the risk for many diseases. Environmental tobacco smoke is a major source of indoor air contaminants; secondhand smoke is estimated to cause approximately 3,000 lung cancer deaths per year among nonsmokers and contributes to more than 35,000 deaths related to cardiovascular disease. Exposure to tobacco smoke in the home is also a risk factor for new cases and increased severity of childhood asthma and has been associated with sudden infant death syndrome. Additionally, dropped cigarettes are the leading cause of residential fire fatalities, leading to more than 1,000 deaths each year.

> *"The politicians' war on smoking makes little sense. Smoking does physical harm, undoubtedly, but alcohol does more. It is also responsible for crime, which tobacco is not."*

The Dangers of Smoking Are Exaggerated

Paul Johnson

In the following viewpoint, Paul Johnson argues that while there are health dangers associated with smoking, the risks are outweighed by the benefits. Smoking has a long and dignified history. It provides, he says, psychological comfort, eases awkward social situations, and may prevent more seriously destructive behaviors. Unlike alcohol, Johnson points out that smoking is seldom associated with criminal acts but instead has a calming effect on individuals, and it is an enjoyable social pastime. Paul Johnson frequently writes for The Spectator, *a British magazine.*

As you read, consider the following questions:

1. Why, according to the author, did the survival of the U.S. colonies depend on the growing of tobacco?

Paul Johnson, "One Last Cigarette before the Firing Squad? Certainly Not!" *Spectator*, vol. 304, no. 9339, August 11, 2007, p. 30. Copyright © 2007 by *The Spectator*. Reproduced by permission of *The Spectator*.

2. The author names several members of the British royal family who have died as a result of tobacco use. Who are they?

3. Why does the author think that politicians prefer to campaign against smoking, rather than against drinking?

I suppose in 100 years' time, perhaps much sooner, no one will smoke. So we will be back where we were before the 16th century, when adventurers like [Sir Walter] Raleigh brought the Red Indian [as Native Americans were known to Europeans of the time] habit of smoking tobacco to Europe. It was one of the points on which he intrigued Queen Elizabeth. 'I can weigh tobacco smoke, Your Grace.' 'Oh no, you can't, Sir Walter.' Then he would produce a small pair of scales, weigh a bit of tobacco, smoke it, then weigh the ashes, 'The difference between the two is the weight of the smoke.' 'Well I never, Sir Walter.' Her successor, James I, hated smoking, wrote a book denouncing it, and would have banned it. But that would have meant losing the duties on imported tobacco, so he dropped his plan. It's odd that Americans have led the campaign to end smoking, now being followed all over the [Western] world. When the first American colonies were founded from England, tobacco was virtually the only crop they learnt how to grow which Europeans wanted to buy. Without it, they could not have survived, and the United States would never have come into existence. Its origins were built on the weed.

Choosing to Smoke

I suspect smoking is one of those indulgencies which, bad in themselves, prevent human beings from doing worse. My friend Vicky, the cartoonist, used to get through 80 fags [cigarettes] a day. He knew it was wrong and, with a great effort of willpower, stopped. But the deprivation increased sharply his already powerful melancholia [depression], and his insomnia, and in due course he took too many sleeping tablets. I gave up smoking 40 years ago, and don't miss it—apparently. But I know many cases where not smoking led to more drinking or eating. [Nineteenth-century British essayist] Charles Lamb used to make this point, for when he 'left off smoking', as he put it, his consumption of gin increased. It is significant that the Jesuits [a Catholic religious order], those clever fellows, never forbade smoking in their order. I believe the licence went back to old Ignatius Gonzaga, their founder, a former soldier who had learned to smoke in sieges. Anyway, when I was at school all the Jesuits smoked, usually pipes, being cheaper. If you went into a Jesuit's room, it stank of tobacco. So did they. One told me, 'Tobacco is essential to a celibate priesthood.' That may be why Catholic priests smoke more, often much more, than Anglican clergymen—nonconformist ministers too. Father Ronald Knox told me his consumption of tobacco rose after his conversion, 'which was to be expected'. He was a fanatical smoker who would have objected strongly to the current persecution, and written against it, even more so than the late [jazz artist] George Melly, as well as [musician] Simon Grey and [painter] David Hockney. [Quarterback] Ronnie Knox, on coming into a strange room, would sniff and say, 'This room smells suspiciously of never having been smoked in.' He thought a smokeless room might carry a curse, 'The Devil lives in Hell but he never smokes.'

Preventing Worse Behaviors

When men are smoking pipes peacefully they are not likely to engage in violence or fornication. Or to be angry, envious or revengeful. [Writer] J.B. Priestley, a tremendous pipe-smoker, used to say, 'Tobacco is incompatible with serious sin.' There is a splendid photo of [Thomas] Carlyle and [Alfred Lord] Tennyson [well-known nineteenth-century literary figures] sitting side by side in Cheyne Row, Chelsea, placidly smoking long white clay pipes. Carlyle said, 'I learnt smoking as a schoolboy. It is the only creature comfort which gives me any satisfac-

"You get time off to give up smoking, it's only fair that we take paid time off to start smoking!"

Cartoon courtesy of Steven Smith.

tion. After working for a long spell, I always have an interlude of tobacco. I get my pipes from Paisley, buying them by the box. I prefer a new pipe. I smoke a new pipe every day, and put the old one out at night on the doorstep, so that some poor man may have it if he wishes.'

Tennyson had a quite different approach. He disliked a new pipe—thought an old one tasted much better. He had a wooden frame for his pipes hanging on the wall, with room for 14. He smoked a different one each day, in order, coming back to the beginning each fortnight. Carlyle thought this very odd, even 'fanatical', adding, 'Tennyson smokes too much anyway.' They differed on other points. Carlyle thought that dry tobacco was stronger and harmful. Tennyson carefully dried his tobacco before smoking, saying, 'It lessens the strength and so does you less harm. The trouble with Carlyle is that he doesn't dry his. But then he smokes too much anyway.'

Setting the Right Atmosphere

Odd to think of how much trouble our forebears once went to, creating the right atmosphere for smoking. They wore frogged velvet smoking-jackets, in dark blue, bottle green or wine, crowned it with square, heavily embroidered caps, often with a gold tassel. Until recently you could buy one in that fine hatters in Jermyn Street. They had special rooms for smoking. There were places in the West End [of London] known as Cigar Divans. Mr Sponge, at the end of his Sporting Tour [*Mr. Sponge's Sporting Tour* is a nineteenth-century British novel], set one up with his beautiful rider-to-hounds wife, Lucy. I suppose clients lay on their velour-covered divan, and puffed luxuriously. When the rich Marquess of Bute had Cardiff Castle completely rebuilt to his taste, he had both a winter and a summer smoking-room.

No doubt smoking is a killer, members of our royal family being notable among its victims. Smoking (of cigars) killed old Edward VII, though eating must have had something to do with it too. Smoking (of cigarettes as well as cigars) killed George V. And smoking (of cigarettes, Craven 'A' Extra Strength) killed George VI. His daughter Princess Margaret was a notorious cigarette smoker too, especially during meals. I once saw her extinguish a fag by plunging it into the middle of a delicious tournedos, at a dinner party given by the then

Papal Nuncio [an ambassador from the Vatican], a famous gourmand and amateur chef. How the archbishop winced! I have heard it said that Queen Victoria, while normally disapproving of tobacco, especially for women, used to smoke a pipe secretly with her friend John Brown when 'on the hill'.

A Widespread Habit

When I first went to the United States half a century ago, one of the things that struck me was seeing ordinary working men, on building sites or driving street-cars, chomping away on big, fat cigars. It was visible proof of how prosperous America was. It shocked me, however, to see Catholic priests smoking them. Walking down Fifth Avenue I spotted a portly fellow, in long clerical skirts and with a biretta perched on his head, with a Churchill-sized Havana in his mouth. Noting my interest, he paused, took out his cigar, and said, 'Don't try to kid me, Mac, I know you're Irish,' and then strode on, laughing.

The politicians' war on smoking makes little sense. Smoking does physical harm, undoubtedly, but alcohol does more. It is also responsible for crime, which tobacco is not. Yet while parliament has been pouring out legislation against smoking, the government over the past decade has made drinking, at all hours and everywhere, much easier, and the consequences are overwhelmingly evident and serious. No doubt the alcohol industry bribes the politicians, both individually and collectively, through the party system. Did not the tobacco industry in its day? Not sufficiently, it seems. Of the motives that drive people to go into politics, the most important is vanity. But following close behind it is the itch for power, especially the power to stop ordinary people from doing what they like, for their own good. So they are sure to turn on drink in the end. After that it will be eating meat. What then? Sex? But before that, I suspect, people will turn on the professional politicians. Oh that I could live to see the day!

> "A growing number of communities, counties, and states are requiring smoke-free environments for nearly all enclosed public places, including all private worksites, restaurants, bars, and casinos."

Secondhand Smoke Is a Serious Problem

Richard Carmona

In the following viewpoint, Richard Carmona argues that exposure to secondhand smoke remains a serious threat to public health, in spite of recent improvements. A growing body of evidence indicates that secondhand smoke causes lung cancer in lifetime nonsmokers, and that the disease process is similar to that of those who smoke. In addition, cardiovascular effects of secondhand smoke, while less than those experienced by smokers, are still significant. And Carmona notes that other health effects still need to be explored. Progress must be made toward a society free of involuntary exposure to secondhand smoke, Carmona asserts. Richard Carmona, a physician, was Surgeon General of the United States from 2002 until 2006.

Richard Carmona, "A Vision for the Future," *The Health Consequences of Involuntary Exposure to Tobacco Smoke: A Report of the Surgeon General*, 2006, pp. 22–24. www .surgeongeneral.gov. Reproduced by permission.

As you read, consider the following questions:

1. How has the behavior of physicians and public health workers changed since the 1964 Surgeon General's report on smoking and health?

2. Who was the first Surgeon General to call attention to the health effects of secondhand smoke?

3. What is cotinine, and where is it found?

This country has experienced a substantial reduction of involuntary exposure to secondhand tobacco smoke in recent decades. Significant reductions in the rate of smoking among adults began even earlier. Consequently, about 80 percent of adults are now nonsmokers, and many adults and children can live their daily lives without being exposed to secondhand smoke. Nevertheless, involuntary exposure to secondhand smoke remains a serious public health hazard. . . .

Children Still Grow Up in Carcinogenic Environments

Multiple major reviews of the evidence have concluded that secondhand smoke is a known human carcinogen, and that exposure to secondhand smoke causes adverse effects, particularly on the cardiovascular system and the respiratory tract and on the health of those exposed, children as well as adults. Unfortunately, reductions in exposure have been slower among young children than among adults during the last decade, as expanding workplace restrictions now protect the majority of adults while homes remain the most important source of exposure for children.

Attitudes Have Changed

Clearly, the social norms regarding secondhand smoke have changed dramatically, leading to widespread support over the past 30 years for a society free of involuntary exposures to tobacco smoke. In the first half of the twentieth century smoking was permitted in almost all public places, including elevators and all types of public transportation. At the time of the 1964 Surgeon General's report on smoking and health, many physicians were still smokers, and the tables in U.S. Public Health Service (PHS) meeting rooms had PHS ashtrays on them. A thick, smoky haze was an accepted part of presentations at large meetings, even at medical conferences and in the hospital environment.

As the adverse health consequences of active smoking became more widely documented in the 1960s, many people began to question whether exposure of nonsmokers to secondhand smoke also posed a serious health risk. This topic was first addressed in this series [*Surgeon General's Report*] by Surgeon General Jesse Steinfeld in the 1972 report to Congress. During the 1970s, policy changes to provide smoke-free environments received more widespread consideration. As the public policy debate grew and expanded in the 1980s, the scientific evidence on the risk of adverse effects from exposure to secondhand smoke was presented in a comprehensive context for the first time by Surgeon General C. Everett Koop in the 1986 report, *The Health Consequences of Involuntary Smoking*.

Nonsmokers Are Clearly at Risk

The ever-increasing momentum for smoke-free indoor environments has been driven by scientific evidence on the health risks of involuntary exposure to secondhand smoke. . . . The growing body of data increases support for the conclusion that exposure to secondhand smoke causes lung cancer in lifetime nonsmokers. . . . The mechanisms by which secondhand smoke causes lung cancer are similar to those that cause lung cancer in active smokers. In the context of the risks from active smoking, the lung cancer risk that secondhand smoke exposure poses to nonsmokers is. . .[proportionate to how much smoke they inhale].

Hearts Can Be Damaged by Secondhand Smoke

Cardiovascular effects of even short exposures to secondhand smoke are readily measurable, and the risks for cardiovascular disease from involuntary smoking appear to be about 50 percent less than the risks for active smokers. Although the risks from secondhand smoke exposures are larger than anticipated, research on the mechanisms by which tobacco smoke exposure affects the cardiovascular system supports the plausibility of the findings. . . .

Since 1986, the attitude of the public toward and the social norms around secondhand smoke exposure have changed dramatically to reflect a growing viewpoint that the involuntary exposure of nonsmokers to secondhand smoke is unacceptable. As a result, increasingly strict public policies to control involuntary exposure to secondhand smoke have been put in place. The need for restrictions on smoking in enclosed public places is now widely accepted in the United States. A growing number of communities, counties, and states are requiring smoke-free environments for nearly all enclosed public places, including all private worksites, restaurants, bars, and casinos.

Questions Multiply As Knowledge Grows

As knowledge about the health risks of secondhand smoke exposure grows, investigators continue to identify additional scientific questions.

- Because active smoking is firmly established as a causal factor of cancer for a large number of sites, and because many scientists assert that there may be no threshold for carcinogenesis from tobacco smoke exposure, researchers hypothesize that people who are exposed to secondhand smoke are likely to be at some risk for the same types of cancers that have been established as smoking-related among active smokers.

Secondhand Smoke Injures Children

In ranking the greatest Christmas presents of my boyhood, the basketball hoop on the garage tops the BB gun and the electric football game. . . .

Only as an adult did I realize the greatest gift actually came a month before the basketball hoop, when my dad quit smoking. . . .

It was a joy growing up in a house with nonsmoking parents. Today, 21 million kids in the United States live in homes where a family member or visitor smokes on a regular basis. Secondhand smoke is blamed for as many as 300,000 respiratory tract infections in children younger than 18 months old. It aggravates hundreds of thousands of kids with asthma, and can lead to worse ailments. . . .

Burt Constable,
"I Wanna Wii, iPod and Parents Who Quit Smoking,"
Daily Herald *(Chicago), December 13, 2007.*

- The potential risks for stroke and subclinical vascular disease from secondhand smoke exposure require additional research.

- There is a need for additional research on the etiologic [having to do with cause or origin] relationship between secondhand smoke exposure and several respiratory health outcomes in adults, including respiratory symptoms, declines in lung function, and adult-onset asthma.

- There is also a need for research to further evaluate the adverse reproductive outcomes and childhood respiratory effects from both prenatal and postnatal exposure to secondhand smoke.

- Further research and improved methodologies are also needed to advance an understanding of the potential effects on cognitive, behavioral, and physical development that might be related to early exposures to secondhand smoke.

As these and other research questions are addressed, the scientific literature documenting the adverse health effects of exposure to secondhand smoke will expand. Over the past 40 years since the release of the landmark 1964 report of the Surgeon General's Advisory Committee on Smoking and Health, researchers have compiled an ever-growing list of adverse health effects caused by exposure to tobacco smoke, with evidence that active smoking causes damage to virtually every organ of the body. Similarly, since the 1986 report, the number of adverse health effects caused by exposure to secondhand smoke has also expanded. Following the format of the electronic database released with the 2004 report, the research findings supporting the conclusions in this report will be accessible in a database that can be found at http://www.cdc.gov/tobacco. With an this expanding base of scientific knowledge, the list of adverse health effects caused by exposure to secondhand smoke will likely increase.

Evidence of Improvement

Biomarker data from the 2005 *Third National Report on Human Exposure to Environmental Chemicals* document great progress since the 1986 report in reducing the involuntary exposure of nonsmokers to secondhand smoke. Between the late 1980s and 2002, the median cotinine level (a metabolite of nicotine) among nonsmokers declined by more than 70 percent. Nevertheless, many challenges remain to maintain the momentum toward universal smoke-free environments. First, there is a need to continue and even improve the surveillance of sources and levels of exposure to secondhand smoke. The data from the 2005 exposure report show that median cotinine levels among children are more than twice those of nonsmoking adults, and non-Hispanic Blacks have levels more than twice those of Mexican Americans and non-Hispanic Whites. The multiple factors related to these disparities in median cotinine levels among nonsmokers need to be identified and addressed. Second, the data from the 2005 exposure report suggest that the scientific community should sustain the current momentum to reduce exposures of nonsmokers to secondhand smoke. Research reviewed in this report indicates that policies creating completely smoke-free environments are the most economical and efficient approaches to providing this protection. Additionally, neither central heating, ventilating, and air conditioning systems nor separately ventilated rooms control exposures to secondhand smoke. Unfortunately, data from the 2005 exposure report also emphasized that young children remain an exposed population. However, more evidence is needed on the most effective strategies to promote voluntary changes in smoking norms and practices in homes and private automobiles. Finally, data on the health consequences of secondhand smoke exposures emphasize the importance of the role of health care professionals in this issue. They must assume a greater, more active involvement in reducing exposures, particularly for susceptible groups. . . .

There is an international consensus that exposure to secondhand smoke poses significant public health risks. The Framework Convention on Tobacco Control recognizes that protecting nonsmokers from involuntary exposures to secondhand smoke in public places should be an integral part of comprehensive national tobacco control policies and programs. Recent changes in national policies in countries such as Italy and Ireland reflect this growing international awareness of the need for additional protection of nonsmokers from involuntary exposures to secondhand smoke. . . .

Protecting Nonsmokers Is a Priority

In 1964, the majority of men and a substantial proportion of women were smokers, and most nonsmokers inevitably must have been involuntary smokers. With the release of the 1986 report, Surgeon General Koop noted that "the right of smokers to smoke ends where their behavior affects the health and well-being of others." As understanding increases regarding health consequences from even brief exposures to secondhand smoke, it becomes even clearer that the health of nonsmokers overall, and particularly the health of children, individuals with existing heart and lung problems, and other vulnerable populations, requires a higher priority and greater protection.

Together, this report and the 2004 report of the Surgeon General, *The Health Consequences of Smoking*, document the extraordinary threat to the nation's health from active and involuntary smoking. The recent reductions in exposures of nonsmokers to secondhand smoke represent significant progress, but involuntary exposures persist in many settings and environments. More evidence is needed to understand why this progress has not been equally shared across all populations and in all parts of this nation. Some states (California, Connecticut, Delaware, Maine, Massachusetts, New York, Rhode Island, and Washington) have met the [U.S. Department of Health and Human Services] *Healthy People 2010* objectives that protect against involuntary exposures to secondhand smoke through recommended policies, regulations, and laws, while many other parts of this nation have not. Evidence presented in this report suggests that these disparities in levels of protection can be reduced or eliminated. Sustained progress toward a society free of involuntary exposures to secondhand smoke should remain a national public health priority.

"[The Surgeon General]. . .absurdly exaggerates the hazards of secondhand
smoke, hoping to generate enough public alarm to banish smokers from every
location outside the home."

The Dangers of Secondhand Smoke are Exaggerated

Jacob Sullum

*In the following viewpoint, Jacob Sullum argues that a public
health official exaggerated the effects of secondhand smoke when
promoting a 2006 report on the subject. Sullum feels that then-
Surgeon General Richard Carmona overemphasized the adverse
effects of brief exposure to secondhand smoke, when in reality
the contact must be heavy and long-term to increase the chance
of developing heart or lung disease. Furthermore, Sullum points
out, there are other explanations that could account for the increases in these diseases. Sullum, a senior editor at* Reason *magazine, is an author and nationally syndicated columnist.*

As you read, consider the following questions:

1. Why is it difficult to measure the effect of cigarette
   smoke on non-smoking bystanders?

Jacob Sullum, "A Pack of Lies," *Reason*, July 5, 2006. Copyright © 2006 by Reason
Foundation, 3415 S. Sepulveda Blvd., Suite 400, Los Angeles, CA 90034, www.reason
.com. Reproduced by permission.

2. What other variables could account for the increase in heart and lung disease among non-smokers?

3. How could data about the effects of secondhand smoke affect the movement toward smoking bans?

According to Surgeon General Richard Carmona, second-hand smoke is so dangerous that you'd be better off if you stopped going to smoky bars and started smoking instead. "Even brief exposure to secondhand smoke," claims the press release that accompanied his new report on the subject, "has immediate adverse effects on the cardiovascular system and increases risk for heart disease and lung cancer."

Among smokers, these diseases take many years to develop. So if you got your health tips from the surgeon general, you'd start smoking a pack a day as a protective measure.

But you may want to look elsewhere for medical advice. Carmona is so intent on promoting smoking bans—a key element of the government's campaign to reduce cigarette consumption—that he absurdly exaggerates the hazards of secondhand smoke, hoping to generate enough public alarm to banish smokers from every location outside the home.

As the report itself makes clear, there is no evidence that brief, transient exposure to secondhand smoke has any effect on your chance of developing heart disease or lung cancer. The studies that link secondhand smoke to these illnesses involve intense, long-term exposure, typically among people who have lived with smokers for decades.

Even in these studies, it's difficult to demonstrate an effect, precisely because the doses of toxins and carcinogens bystanders passively absorb are much smaller than the doses absorbed by smokers, probably amounting to a fraction of a cigarette a day. Not surprisingly, the epidemiological studies cited by the surgeon general's report find that the increases in lung cancer and heart disease risks associated with long-term exposure to secondhand smoke are small, on the order of 20 to 30 percent. Among smokers, by contrast, the risk of heart disease is between 100 and 300 percent higher, while the risk of lung cancer is about 900 percent higher.

Because the associations found in the secondhand smoke studies are so weak, it's impossible to rule out alternative explanations, such as unreported smoking or other lifestyle variables that independently raise disease risks. Although the surgeon general's report concludes such factors are unlikely to entirely account for the observed associations, the truth is we don't know for sure and probably never will, given the limitations of epidemiology and the difficulty of measuring low-level risks.

Reasonable people can disagree about the meaning of these ambiguous data, and it's not surprising that supporters of smoking bans like Carmona are inclined to see a clear causal relationship, while opponents (like me) are inclined to be more skeptical. But there is no excuse for the kind of scare mongering in which Carmona engaged when he implied that you could drop dead from the slightest whiff of tobacco smoke.

Even supporters of smoking bans, such as longtime anti-smoking activist Michael Siegel, faulted Carmona for gilding the lily (blackening the lung?) by saying things such as, "There is NO risk-free level of secondhand smoke exposure." This position contradicts the basic toxicological principle that the dose makes the poison. Since it's hard to measure even the health consequences of heavy, long-term exposure to secondhand smoke, how could one possibly demonstrate an effect from, say, a few molecules? "No risk-free level" is an article of faith, not a scientific statement.

Speaking of which, Carmona was at pains to say he was merely summarizing the science, not making policy recommendations, even though he emphasized that smoking bans are the only way to eliminate the "serious public health hazard" posed by secondhand smoke. He is right about this much:

Research Must Address Confounding Factors

On average, women live longer than men. Any study on longevity has to account for this fact. This is called a confounder . . . Any study of longevity . . . which doesn't take this confounder into account will be very inaccurate. For instance, when studying the longevity of smokers, it's important to adjust for the gender difference, and adjust for the percentage of men and women in the study.

Sound complicated? It gets worse. Poor people die sooner than rich people. Black people die sooner than white people, even when adjusting for the income confounder. People in some countries live longer than people in others. So if an impoverished black male smoker in Uruguay dies before reaching the median age, is it because of his income, race, gender, smoking, or nationality?

Fact: When studying the effects of tobacco exposure, either to the smoker or to those around him, confounders include age, allergies, nationality, race, medications, compliance with medications, education, gas heating and cooking, gender, socioeconomic status, exposure to other chemicals, occupation, use of alcohol, use of marijuana, consumption of saturated fat and other dietary considerations, family history of cancer and domestic radon exposure, to name a few.

Fact: When studying the effects of SHS [Secondhand Smoke] on children confounders include most of the above, plus breast feeding, crowding, day care and school attendance, maternal age, maternal symptoms of depression, parental allergies, parental respiratory symptoms and prematurity.

A study that does not account for *all* of these factors is likely to be very inaccurate, and is probably worthless.

Dave Hitt, "The Facts," www.davehitt.com.

The issue of what the government should do about second-hand smoke is independent from the issue of exactly how risky it is. Whether smoking bans are a good idea is a question not of science but of values, of whether we want to live in a country where a majority forcibly imposes its preferences on everyone else or one where there is room for choice and diversity.

> *"Whatever form it's in, tobacco is dangerous and smokeless tobacco is a direct assault on oral tissue, increasing the user's risk for disease."*

Smokeless Tobacco Is Harmful to Human Health

Business Wire

In the following viewpoint, Business Wire *reports on dental experts' criticism of new smokeless tobacco products. Tobacco companies are promoting the products as safe alternatives to cigarettes, a claim which dental professors and other experts strongly contradict, saying that tobacco is dangerous in any form. Furthermore, they feel that the FDA should regulate the manufacture and marketing of these smokeless products in the same way that they regulate cigarettes.*

As you read, consider the following questions:

1. For what reasons are tobacco users attracted to smokeless tobacco products?
2. Why do dental experts say that smokeless tobacco is harmful?

Business Wire, "Dental Experts Blast Tobacco Companies for Expanding Smokeless Product Lines, Urge Congress to Pass Bills Giving FDA Oversight of Tobacco Products," April 30, 2008. Reproduced by permission.

3. What cancer-causing agents can be found in smokeless tobacco?

New tobacco products being test marketed by U.S. tobacco companies will likely discourage users from quitting and will lure non-users, especially young people, to adopt a nicotine habit, warns Dr. Jed Jacobson, chief science officer of Delta Dental of Michigan, Ohio, Indiana, and Tennessee (Delta Dental). He said the products, known as snus (pronounced "snoose"), are not safe and should not be used by consumers.

Jacobson, and Dr. Joan McGowan, associate professor at the University of Michigan School of Dentistry, say the new product lines—part of the tobacco industry's growth strategy to counter declining smoking rates and smoking bans—should spur Congress to pass proposed legislation that would grant the U.S. Food and Drug Administration (FDA) broad authority to regulate tobacco products.

Snus is a Swedish type of smokeless tobacco that is packaged in teabag-like pouches that a user sticks between the upper lip and gum. They may appeal to smokers whose habits have been curtailed by no smoking laws or who don't like the idea of spitting out traditional chewing tobacco or snuff. Tobacco companies, and some proponents of the product, say snus is less harmful than cigarette smoking. Test marketing of the product is expanding to more metropolitan areas in the U.S. this spring.

"Tobacco companies are touting snus as a safe alternative to smoking but their claims are unproven, misleading, and, frankly, suspect," said Jacobson. "Without rigorous oversight by a regulatory agency, American consumers will never know the full truth about the health risks of any tobacco product."

"Whatever form it's in, tobacco is dangerous and smokeless tobacco is a direct assault on oral tissue, increasing the user's risk for disease," said McGowan. "It's time to put an end to the tobacco industry's disregard for public health by requir-

Who Uses Smokeless Tobacco?

Data from the US Centers for Disease Control and Prevention (CDC) showed that among adults aged 18 and older in 2004, about 3% of people (6% of men and less than 1% of women) were current users of smokeless tobacco.

Rates among young people, however, are higher. According to the CDC's 2005 survey, about 14% of male high school students and 2% of female high school students were using smokeless tobacco. The CDC 2004 Tobacco Survey reported that, of middle school students, 4% of the boys and 2% of the girls reported using smokeless tobacco at least once in the 30 days before the survey. Teens who use smokeless tobacco are more likely to smoke later.

Certain factors seem to be linked to whether or not young people will use tobacco. They include:

- peer pressure
- local lifestyles and fashions
- general attitudes toward authority
- economic conditions
- examples set by teachers and school staff
- presence of gangs
- use of illegal drugs and alcohol

American Cancer Society,
"Smokeless Tobacco and How to Quit."
www.cancer.org.

ing FDA approval over the manufacture and marketing of current and new tobacco products."

She continued, "While sales of cigarettes have been on the decline, sales of smokeless products have been growing for the past several years, and cigarette companies are now capitalizing on this trend. The increased use of smokeless tobacco products should be seen as a major public health problem requiring collaborative efforts on the part of dental health professionals, school personnel, parents, and community organizations to educate our children on the dangers of all these tobacco products and addiction."

The landmark bi-partisan bills (Senate Bill 625 and House Bill 1108), known as the Family Smoking Prevention and Tobacco Control Act, recently passed out of committee. They may go to the full Senate and House for consideration before the Memorial Day recess.

Among other things, the proposed legislation requires tobacco companies to disclose detailed information about their products and marketing efforts, authorizes the FDA to require changes in current and future tobacco products to make them safer, and prohibits tobacco companies from making any explicit or implicit health claims.

More About Smokeless Tobacco

- Smokeless tobacco is available as chewing tobacco, snuff (including snus), and dissolvable tablets.

- Snus was first developed in Sweden, which is the only country in the European Union where its use is legal. Some studies have shown that Swedish-produced snus contains lower levels of cancer-causing chemicals than those found in cigarettes or U.S.-produced snuff.

- Recently published data suggests that the use of Swedish snus doubles the user's risk of pancreatic cancer.

- "Snus" means snuff in Swedish. Without regulation, U.S. tobacco companies can brand any form of smokeless tobacco as snus.

- A recent study by researchers at the University of Minnesota concluded that smokeless tobacco is not a safe substitute for smoking. It found that users of smokeless tobacco had a similar exposure to one of tobacco's most potent cancer-causing agents, known as NNK.

- According to the National Cancer Institute (NCI), smokeless tobacco contains 28 cancer-causing agents, including formaldehyde (the same chemical used in embalming), butanol (an industrial solvent and alternative fuel), and polonium-210 and uranium-235 (both used in nuclear weapons).

- In addition, the NCI also reports that the amount of nicotine absorbed from smokeless tobacco is 3 to 4 times the amount delivered by a cigarette. Nicotine is absorbed more slowly from smokeless tobacco than from cigarettes and stays in the bloodstream for a longer time.

- According to the U.S. Centers for Disease Control, an estimated 3 percent of adults are current smokeless tobacco users. In addition, 13.6 percent of all boys in U.S. high schools and 2.2 percent of high school girls use smokeless tobacco products.

- Sales of one category of smokeless tobacco are soaring. The Federal Trade Commission reported that sales of moist snuff in the U.S. more than doubled in volume from 1986 to 2005.

> *"Tobacco harm reduction. . .involves the use of alternative sources of nicotine, including modern smokeless tobacco (ST) products, by those smokers who are unable or unwilling to quit tobacco and nicotine entirely."*

Smokeless Tobacco Is Less Harmful to Human Health Than Smoking

Brad Rodu and William T. Godshall

In the following viewpoint, the authors argue that the dangers of smoking tobacco are widely known and that smoking cessation is the healthiest choice. However, they say, many severely addicted people are unable to quit. One alternative is to substitute a safer source of nicotine, such as a modern smokeless tobacco (ST) product, for tobacco products that are inhaled, in order to reduce the harm caused by nicotine addiction. They claim that a substantial body of scientific research supports harm reduction as a solution for persons who are addicted to nicotine and have been unable to quit smoking. Brad Rodu holds the Endowed Chair for

Brad Rodu and William T. Godshall, "Tobacco Harm Reduction: An Alternative Cessation Strategy for Inveterate Smokers," *Harm Reduction Journal*, vol. 3, no. 37, December 21, 2006. Reproduced by permission.

Tobacco Harm Reduction Research at the University of Louisville School of Medicine, and William T. Godshall is the founder and executive director of Smokefree Pennsylvania.

As you read, consider the following questions:

1. How many people die each year from smoking-related illnesses?
2. Why are nicotine replacement medications an impractical solution for some smokers?
3. How does the Institute of Medicine define a tobacco harm reduction product?

According to the Centers for Disease Control and Prevention (CDC), about 45 million Americans continue to smoke, even after one of the most intense public health campaigns in history, now over 40 years old. Some 438,000 smokers die from smoking-related diseases each year, including lung and other cancers, cardiovascular disorders and pulmonary diseases.

There is clear evidence that smokers of any age can reap substantial health benefits by quitting. In fact, no other single public health effort is likely to achieve a benefit comparable to large-scale smoking cessation. Surveys document that most smokers would like to quit, and many have made repeated efforts to do so. However, conventional smoking cessation approaches require nicotine-addicted smokers to abstain from tobacco and nicotine entirely (as discussed later, use of nicotine replacement medications is limited to 10–12 weeks, per labels required by federal regulations). Many smokers are unable—or at least unwilling—to achieve this goal, and so they continue smoking in the face of impending adverse health consequences. In effect, the status quo in smoking cessation presents smokers with just two unpleasant alternatives: quit or die.

A Realistic Alternative: Harm Reduction

There is a third choice for smokers: tobacco harm reduction. It involves the use of alternative sources of nicotine, including modern smokeless tobacco (ST) products, by those smokers who are unable or unwilling to quit tobacco and nicotine entirely. The history of tobacco harm reduction may be traced back to 1974, with the publication of a special article in the *Lancet* [a leading British medical journal] by British tobacco addiction research expert Michael A.H. Russell. Citing the "high dependence-producing potency and the universal appeal of the effects of nicotine" on smokers, Russell likened "harsher restrictive measures" and "intensification" of anti-smoking efforts to "flogging a dead horse harder." Russell believed that "the goal of abstinence and the abolition of all smoking is unrealistic and doomed to fail."

Six years later Russell's research group compared nicotine absorption rates from various tobacco products, which led them to suggest that nasal snuff use could serve as an effective substitute for cigarette smoking. This article was cited shortly thereafter by a short letter in a leading American medical journal. Russell et al. published follow-up studies on nasal snuff in 1981 and on an oral ST product in 1985. Lynn Kozlowski, a prominent American smoking and nicotine addiction expert at Penn State University, noted in 1984 and 1989 that ST products conferred fewer risks to users and therefore might serve as effective substitutes for cigarettes. In 1994 oral pathologist Brad Rodu and epidemiologist Philip Cole from the University of Alabama at Birmingham made quantitative comparisons of the risks from oral ST use and smoking in a series of studies. Some of that work was summarized in a 1995 ACSH [American Council on Science and Health] publication.

A substantial body of research over the past decade has been transformed into the scientific and medical foundation for tobacco harm reduction, the substitution of safer sources

Harm Reduction Can Work

A recent Institute of Medicine (IOM) report concluded that risk reduction through potential exposure reduction products (PREPs) is feasible. They also stated that the science base for harm reduction needs to be developed and then translated into a comprehensive policy framework that includes a well-designed program for public health education and an integrated program of federal regulation.

According to the IOM definition of a PREP, "a product is harm reducing if it lowers total tobacco related mortality and morbidity even though use of that product may involve continued exposure to tobacco related toxicants." The IOM committee, the World Health Organization Scientific Advisory Council on Tobacco (SACTob) and others, have recognized that there are extraordinary opportunities and extraordinary risks for harm reduction strategies.

Lombardi Comprehensive Cancer Center.
http://lombardi.georgetown.edu.

of nicotine, including tobacco products, by those smokers who are unable or unwilling to achieve nicotine and tobacco abstinence. In 2001 the Institute of Medicine, a subsidiary of the National Academy of Sciences, provided a now widely accepted definition of a harm reduction product as "harm reducing if it lowers total tobacco related mortality and morbidity even though use of that product may involve continued exposure to tobacco related toxicants. . . ."

A Strategy with Many Benefits

Tobacco harm reduction empowers smokers to gain control over the consequences of their nicotine addiction. At its simplest it is nonintrusive and solely educational, and therefore has a strong moral rationale. The strategy is cost-effective and accessible today to almost all smokers. But its implementation will require rethinking of conventional tobacco control policies and their premises.

The ACSH believes that the following actions will benefit smokers:

1. *Agencies of the federal government (most notably the Office of the Surgeon General) and health promotion organizations (such as the American Cancer Society and the Mayo Clinic) should discontinue the campaign of misinformation that irresponsibly misrepresents the scientific information about and use of ST products.* They endanger their reputations as sources of trusted health information by providing messages about ST products that are neither accurate nor credible. The campaign of misinformation should be replaced with an educational program that emphasizes the differential risks of all forms of tobacco use.

2. *Regulatory restrictions on the manufacture and sale of nicotine replacement medications should be revised.* Nicotine is addictive, but it plays little or no role in the development of most smoking-related diseases. Manufacturers of nicotine replacement medications should be permitted to sell higher doses of the drug within flavor/ delivery systems that are satisfying and enjoyable for smokers at costs that are competitive with cigarettes. In addition, smokers should be informed that permanent use of NRT [nicotine replacement therapy] is vastly safer than continuing to smoke. This could be accomplished by new labels on NRT packaging and additional labels on cigarette packs: "Notice: Nicotine does not cause cancer, heart diseases or emphysema."

3. *Manufacturers of tobacco products should follow the lead of British American Tobacco (BAT) and acknowledge that*

ST use is vastly safer than smoking. BAT has openly admitted that oral ST products are safer than cigarettes, and this company is actively engaged in test-marketing Swedish snus [an ST product] in Sweden, Norway and South Africa. At the press date of this report, cigarette manufacturers in the U.S. have introduced ST products in limited test markets, but they have made no statements regarding differential health risks. This is unacceptable, given the state of the science documented in this report.

4. *Any federal legislation that addresses the regulation of tobacco should include provisions that adequately reflect the differences in risks between combustible tobacco products and ST products or NRT.* This includes careful review of current proposals before Congress to ensure that the legislation is written to regulate the labeling and marketing of products based on their risks. The goal should be to give users of tobacco the necessary information they need to understand the differences between various tobacco and nicotine products so they can make the appropriate health choices and decisions.

5. *Pending enactment of more comprehensive regulation, the U.S. Congress should repeal the federally-mandated warning that now appears on ST products:* "This product is not a safe alternative to cigarettes." This warning not only misleads smokers; it may send a message to ST users that they might as well smoke. The warning should be replaced with the following, which would appear. . .with cigarette packages—"Warning: Smokeless tobacco use has risks, but cigarette smoking is far more dangerous. Quitting tobacco entirely is ideal, but switching from cigarettes to ST can reduce greatly the health risks to smokers and those around them." Placement of this warning with cigarettes ensures that it reaches the target audience, continuing smokers.

6. *State legislatures should follow the lead of Kentucky and establish rational risk-based tax policies for tobacco products.* In 2005 the Commonwealth of Kentucky enacted an excise tax structure for cigarettes and ST products that was based on differential risks. The final bill stated: "The General Assembly recognizes that increasing taxes on tobacco products should reduce consumption, and therefore result in healthier lifestyles for Kentuckians. The relative taxes on tobacco products proposed in this section reflect the growing data from scientific studies suggesting that although smokeless tobacco poses some risks, those health risks are significantly less than the risks posed by other forms of tobacco products. Moreover, the General Assembly acknowledges that some in the public health community recognize that tobacco harm reduction should be a complementary public health strategy regarding tobacco products. Taxing tobacco products according to relative risk is a rational tax policy and may well serve the public health goal of reducing smoking-related mortality and morbidity and lowering health care costs associated with tobacco-related disease."

"We cannot be satisfied when more than 21 percent of high school seniors still smoke. Half who continue to smoke will die prematurely as a result."

Efforts to Reduce Teen Smoking Have Stalled

William V. Corr

In the following viewpoint, William V. Corr argues that efforts to reduce teen smoking rates have stalled, while an unacceptably high number of teens continue to smoke. Claiming that recent cuts in state spending on tobacco prevention and cessation programs, increased spending by the tobacco companies on marketing, and the stabilization of cigarette prices have all contributed to the lack of progress toward reduction of teen smoking, Corr believes the U.S. Food and Drug Administration should have the authority to regulate manufacture and marketing of tobacco products. He also maintains that states should increase tobacco taxes and fund programs aimed at preventing teen smoking. William V. Corr is executive director of the Campaign for Tobacco-Free Kids.

William V. Corr, "New Survey Confirms High School Smoking Declines Have Stalled; Congress, States Must Step up Tobacco Prevention Efforts," Campaign for Tobacco-Free Kids, December 11, 2007. www.tobaccofreekids.org. Reproduced by permission.

As you read, consider the following questions:

1. What does the author say has recently happened to smoking rates among tenth, eleventh, and twelfth graders?
2. What actions could the federal government take to reduce teen smoking, according to the author?
3. Historically, what impact has the price of cigarettes had on smoking rates?

L ike other recent surveys, the 2007 *Monitoring the Future* survey released [recently] by the National Institute on Drug Abuse shows that the nation's progress in reducing youth smoking has stalled or slowed to a crawl. It is encouraging that the survey found that smoking declined among 8th graders from 2006 to 2007, the first statistically significant decline in that age group in four years. However, it is troubling and bad news for the nation's health that, for the fourth year in a row, the survey found no statistically significant change in smoking rates for 10th and 12th graders.

A Troubling Lack of Progress

There is no question that we know how to dramatically reduce youth smoking as evidenced by the fact that smoking rates (the percentage who have smoked in the past 30 days) have declined by 66 percent among 8th graders, 54 percent among 10th graders and 41 percent among 12th graders since peaking in the mid-1990s. But the lack of progress in recent years is a clear warning to elected officials at all levels to resist complacency and redouble efforts to implement proven measures to reduce tobacco use. It is unacceptable to stand still in the fight against tobacco use, the number one preventable cause of death in the United States. We cannot be satisfied when more than 21 percent of high school seniors still smoke. Half who continue to smoke will die prematurely as a result.

State Excise Tax Rates on Cigarettes

(January 1, 2007)

State	Tax Rate (¢ per pack)	Rank	State	Tax Rate (¢ per pack)	Rank
Alabama	42.5	40	Nebraska	64	31
Alaska	180	7	Nevada	80	26
Arizona	200	4	New Hampshire	80	26
Arkansas	59	33	New Jersey	257.5	1
California	87	24	New Mexico	91	23
Colorado	84	25	New York	150	13
Connecticut	151	11	North Carolina	35	44
Delaware	55	36	North Dakota	44	39
Florida	33.9	45	Ohio	125	16
Georgia	37	41	Oklahoma	103	19
Hawaii	160	10	Oregon	118	18
Idaho	57	34	Pennsylvania	135	15
Illinois	98	22	Rhode Island	246	2
Indiana	55.5	35	South Carolina	7	51
Iowa	36	42	South Dakota	53	38
Kansas	79	28	Tennessee	20	48
Kentucky	30	46	Texas	141	14
Louisiana	36	42	Utah	69.5	30
Maine	200	4	Vermont	179	8
Maryland	100	20	Virginia	30	46
Massachusetts	151	11	Washington	202.5	3
Michigan	200	4	West Virginia	55	36
Minnesota	123	17	Wisconsin	77	29
Mississippi	18	49	Wyoming	60	32
Missouri	17	50	Dist. of Columbia	100	20
Montana	170	9	U.S. Median	80.0	

TAKEN FROM: Federation of Tax Administrators, www.taxadmin.org.

The *Monitoring the Future* survey follows other recent surveys showing that smoking declines have stalled among both youth and adults after nearly a decade of progress. The Centers for Disease Control and Prevention (CDC) recently reported that 20.8 percent of U.S. adults smoked in 2006, about the same as the 20.9 percent who smoked in 2005 and 2004.

What's Needed Is Leadership

Science and experience have identified proven solutions that can continue—indeed, accelerate—our nation's progress in reducing smoking. What's needed is the political leadership to aggressively implement them. Just this year, landmark reports by the Institute of Medicine of the National Academy of Sciences and the President's Cancer Panel have agreed on the steps that Congress and the states must take to significantly reduce and eventually eliminate the tobacco epidemic:

- Congress should enact long-overdue legislation granting the U.S. Food and Drug Administration authority over tobacco products, including the authority to regulate the contents of tobacco products and to restrict tobacco marketing that appeals to children and misleads consumers. Congress should also significantly increase the federal cigarette tax, as called for in pending legislation to fund the State Children's Health Insurance Program, and fund a national public education campaign.

- The states must further increase tobacco taxes, enact comprehensive smoke-free workplace laws and adequately fund tobacco prevention programs at levels recommended by the CDC.

Why Progress Has Stalled

According to the CDC, several factors have contributed to the recent stalling of progress:

- Between 2002 and 2005, states cut funding for tobacco prevention and cessation programs by 28 percent. While funding has increased somewhat since, only three states (Maine, Delaware and Colorado) currently fund tobacco prevention programs at CDC-recommended levels despite the fact all the states combined collect nearly $25 billion a year in revenue from the tobacco settlement and tobacco taxes. At the national level, the American Legacy Foundation [created as part of the 1998 tobacco companies' settlement with 46 states] had to reduce its highly successful truth® public education media campaign because most of its funding under the 1998 tobacco settlement ended after 2003.

• While states cut funding for tobacco prevention, tobacco marketing expenditures have skyrocketed since the 1998 state tobacco settlement. From 1998 to 2005, tobacco marketing expenditures nearly doubled from $6.9 billion to $13.4 billion, according to the most recent Federal Trade Commission report on tobacco marketing.

• Tobacco prices have also played a critical role. From 1997 to 2002, when youth and adult smoking rates declined significantly, the average retail price of a pack of cigarettes increased by 91 percent as a result of the tobacco settlement and cigarette tax increases. Since 2002, cigarette prices have barely increased, and smoking declines have subsequently stalled. Cigarette prices have been stable because the tobacco companies currently spend more than 80 percent of their marketing dollars on price discounts that counteract the effects of state cigarette tax increases. The tobacco companies have done this because they know that higher cigarette prices are one of the most effective ways to reduce smoking, especially among kids.

The Cost of Complacence

Tobacco use kills more than 400,000 Americans and costs the nation nearly $100 billion in health care bills each year. While our nation has made remarkable progress in reducing smoking, the battle is far from won. Political complacency and the tobacco companies' aggressive marketing threaten a reversal of our progress. Our challenge today is to summon the political will to combat the tobacco epidemic as aggressively as the tobacco companies continue to market their deadly and addictive products.

"Researchers don't know exactly why the decline in smoking rates resumed this year, but they say it's an important development."

Teen Smoking Rates Have Declined

Dave Gershman

In the following viewpoint, Dave Gershman reports that teen smoking rates, as measured by the Monitoring the Future *survey, have declined. Although the reasons for the decline are not clear, the author cites the decline as an important development because smoking is still the leading cause of preventable death in the United States. The decline in teen smoking, he points out, is part of an overall reduction in drug and alcohol use among teens. Dave Gershman writes for the* Ann Arbor News *(Michigan).*

As you read, consider the following questions:

1. How many students were included in the *Monitoring the Future* survey?

2. Who conducts the *Monitoring the Future* survey, on which this article is based?

3. What percentage of eighth and tenth graders are daily smokers, according to the *Monitoring the Future* survey? How big a change is this from the previous year?

Cigarette smoking among teenagers dropped this year, as did their use of some illicit drugs with the exception of Ecstasy, which is showing signs of making a comeback, according to an annual survey by University of Michigan [U-M] researchers.

Results of the survey offered particularly good news in the battle against teenage smoking. Smoking rates had been dropping since the mid-1990s, but that drop came to a halt last year as the proportion of students who reported being daily smokers held steady. This year, the proportion of daily smokers dropped again.

Fewer Smokers Will Mean Fewer Deaths

"That should eventually translate into many fewer illnesses and premature deaths for this generation of young people," Lloyd Johnston, the research scientist at U-M who is the principal investigator for the study, said in a statement.

Now in its 33rd year, the *Monitoring the Future* survey was given in 2007 to 48,025 students in the eighth, 10th and 12th grades in 403 schools across the country. U-M's Institute for Social Research conducts the study for the federal government. The latest findings were released [December 11, 2007] in Washington and President [George W.] Bush hailed the results at a press conference.

The proportion of 8th graders who reported being daily smokers dropped to 3 percent, down nearly 1 percentage point from last year. Among 10th graders, 7.2 percent reported being daily smokers, down about half a percentage point from last year. Among 12th graders, 12.3 percent reported being daily smokers, which is nearly the same as last year.

Researchers don't know exactly why the decline in smoking rates resumed this year, but they say it's an important de-

Tobacco Control Programs Work

States that have made larger investments in comprehensive tobacco control programs have seen cigarette sales drop more than twice as much as in the United States as a whole, and smoking prevalence among adults and youth has declined faster as spending for tobacco control programs increased. In Florida, between 1998 and 2002, a comprehensive prevention program anchored by an aggressive youth-oriented health communications campaign reduced smoking rates among middle school students by 50% and among high school students by 35%. Other states, such as Maine, New York, and Washington, have seen 45% to 60% reductions in youth smoking rates with sustained comprehensive statewide programs.

Centers For Disease Control and Prevention,
"Best Practices for Tobacco Control Programs," 2007.

velopment. Smoking is still the leading preventable cause of death and disease in the country, said Johnston.

A Steady Decline

Overall, the use of drugs and alcohol declined slightly in all three grades of teenagers this year, continuing a long-term downward trend that—like the decrease in smoking—also began in the mid-1990s.

Graham Lapp, a 16-year-old reading a book at a restaurant in the Kerrytown Shops [in Ann Arbor], said he wasn't surprised by the survey results, at least when it comes to Ann Arbor teenagers.

"There's not a lot of pressure in Ann Arbor (to use substances)," he said. "Here, there's a lot of stuff to do and you don't have to. You can. It's readily available, but it's up to you."

The proportion of eighth graders reporting they had used an illicit drug during the previous 12 months prior to taking the survey was 13 percent in 2007, down from a peak of 24 percent in 1996. Among 10th graders, 28 percent reported having used an illicit drug, down from a peak of 39 percent in 1997. Among 12th graders, 36 percent reported having used an illicit drug, down from a peak of 42 percent in 1997.

Commitment Pays

Bush pointed to his administration's commitment in 2002 to reduce drug use among young people by 25 percent in five years. He said the strategy to cut the supply of drugs entering the country and fight the demand for drugs with prevention and treatment programs has had success.

"One exception to this trend is a rise in the abuse of certain prescription painkillers," he noted, according to the text of his remarks distributed by the White House. "This is troubling, and we're going to continue to confront the challenge. Yet the overall direction is hopeful."

At least one in every 20 high school students has tried the powerful narcotic painkiller OxyContin in the past year, according to the survey. Use of the drug in 2007 was slightly higher than in 2002, the first year the drug was included in the survey.

Ecstasy also is showing signs of being on the rebound among older teenagers. The study found 3.5 percent of 10th graders and 4.5 percent of 12th graders reported using Ecstasy at least once in the year before being surveyed.

"These prevalence rates are not very high yet but there is evidence here of this drug beginning to make a comeback," said Johnston. "Young people are coming to see its use as less dangerous than did their predecessors as recently as 2004, and that is a warning signal that the increase in use may continue."

Marijuana is still the most widely used drug, though its use continued to drop among eighth graders. Use of amphetamines and the prescription drug Ritalin also continued to drop somewhat, while the use of drugs like cocaine held steady.

For alcohol use, the study found 16 percent of eighth graders, 33 percent of 10th graders, and 44 percent of 12th graders reported that they drank alcohol at least once in the 30 days before being surveyed.

In Ann Arbor, local trends generally mirror the national picture, though the school district is taking action based on the results of a different survey of its students last year.

Ann Arbor 12th graders reported that they had tried marijuana and had five drinks in a row within two weeks of the survey at rates greater than the national averages.

"While our cigarette use is definitely below the national average we are concerned a bit about our alcohol and drug use, which are being addressed at the high school level in a variety of ways," said Liz Margolis, the school district spokeswoman.

Periodical Bibliography

The following articles have been selected to supplement the diverse views in this chapter.

Catherine Bass and Adam Long	"Chronic Disease Trends, Their Drivers, and Employer-Driven Solutions," *Managed Care Outlook*, February 1, 2008.
Alex Beam	"Where There's Smoke. . .There's Dr. Siegel," *Boston Globe*, November 13, 2007.
Salynn Boyles	"Report Links Teen Smoking, Depression," *Web MD*, October 23, 2007.
William V. Corr	"New Survey Confirms High School Smoking Declines Have Stalled: Congress, States Must Step Up Tobacco Prevention Efforts," *U.S. Newswire*, December 11, 2007.
The Economist	"How to Save a Billion Lives," March 23, 2008.
Sam Elatrash	"Snus for Health: Imperial Tobacco's New Smokeless Product Divides the Industry's Critics," *Montreal Mirror*, December 25, 2007.
Lindsay Lyon	"The Hazard in Hookah Smoke: Water Pipes Seem Safer Than Cigarettes—But May Be Worse," *U.S. News & World Report*, January 28, 2008.
Oncology News International	"President's Panel Urges Changes to Cut Obesity, Smoking Deaths," September 1, 2007.
Anna Quindlen	"Killing the Consumer," *Newsweek*, October 1, 2007.
Tara C. Walker	"What Is It Worth to You? Blacks Pay the Consequences of Smoking in More Ways Than One," *Black Enterprise*, September 2007.
Kelly Wiese	"Suit: Cigarette Makers Targeted Poor Blacks in St. Louis," *Daily Record*, January 14, 2008.

OPPOSING
VIEWPOINTS®
SERIES

CHAPTER 2

How Can Tobacco Use Be Reduced?

Chapter Preface

As health care costs associated with tobacco-related illnesses have grown, attention has increasingly focused on various ways governments, as well as non-governmental organizations, can intervene to prevent or reduce the use of tobacco. Organizations in the United States, such as the American Cancer Society and the Centers for Disease Control and Prevention (CDC), and internationally, such as the World Health Organization and the World Bank, have all supported research demonstrating that tobacco control is a good investment and wise public policy. In many places around the world, their efforts have led to significant reductions in the rate of smoking. Research has also shown that the impact of such programs increases over time.

In the United States, the CDC has defined comprehensive tobacco control as "a coordinated effort to establish smoke-free policies and social norms, to promote and assist tobacco users to quit, and to prevent initiation of tobacco use." In states that have implemented comprehensive tobacco control programs, cigarette sales have fallen at twice the rate as in the rest of the United States. Smoking rates among adults and youth in tobacco control states have declined faster than the rate of spending for tobacco control has increased.

California, the state with the longest running comprehensive tobacco control program, has achieved the greatest success. Between 1988 and 2006, adult smoking rates declined from 22.7 percent to 13.3 percent. These declines have been accompanied by reduced incidence of deaths resulting from lung cancer and heart disease, with lung cancer diagnoses declining four times faster than in the nation as a whole. According to the CDC, California, because of its commitment to comprehensive tobacco control, could become the first state in which lung cancer is no longer the leading cause of cancer fatalities.

While California's success is exemplary, tobacco control interventions vary considerably from one locale to another. With a variety of approaches to choose from, programs may focus on protecting the public from exposure to secondhand smoke; promoting smoking cessation; or preventing youth from starting to smoke through advertising or education. They may raise the per-unit cost of cigarettes, or ban smoking in workplaces and public venues through law or regulation. The combination of educational, clinical, regulatory, economic, and social strategies is what makes a tobacco control program comprehensive. The goal is to achieve changes in behavior, and eventually to achieve improvements in health, by influencing social norms and economic incentives on multiple fronts at the same time.

Should cigarette taxes be increased? Should smoking be banned in public places? Should tobacco control efforts focus on children or on adults? These are the kinds of questions that must be asked by any community as it seeks to enact policies that reduce the health care costs associated with tobacco use.

| "*Tobacco [tax increases] are probably the single most cost-effective intervention for adult health in the world.*"

Governments Should Tax Tobacco to Save Lives

Prabhat Jha

In the following viewpoint, Prabhat Jha argues that governments must take tobacco seriously as a leading cause of death of adults worldwide, and that the most effective way to reduce deaths due to smoking is to impose heavy taxes on tobacco. Most smokers become addicted when they're young and later regret their decisions, and most adults who smoke say they would like to quit. Taxing tobacco, the author claims, is a proven effective way of reducing tobacco use. It lowers consumption and increases revenues that can be used to fight poverty or provide health care services. Prabhat Jha is a professor of health and development at the University of Toronto.

As you read, consider the following questions:

1. What does the author say is the leading preventable cause of death in Western countries?

2. According to the author, how does smoking impact the chances that a person will die of tuberculosis in India?

Prabhat Jha, "Death and Tobacco Taxes," *Project Syndicate*, 2007. www.project-syndicate.org. Reproduced by permission.

3. How does the tobacco industry aid smuggling, according to the author?

A global killer is ripping through the world's poorer countries largely unchecked. Within 25 years, it will cause 10 million deaths a year worldwide—more than malaria, maternal deaths, childhood infections and diarrhea combined.

An Epidemic of Premature Deaths

Over half of the dead will be aged 30 to 69, losing about 25 years of life expectancy. The culprit? Tobacco. The same addiction that became the top preventable cause of death in Western countries has made big inroads in developing countries. Smoking killed 100 million people in the 20th century, mostly in developed countries. On current trends smoking will kill about 1 billion people in the 21st century, mostly in developing countries.

In India, smoking triples the risk of death from tuberculosis in men and women and may even contribute to the spread of tuberculosis to others. About 1 million people per year will soon die from smoking in China and India. Perhaps 150 million young adults will be killed by tobacco in these two countries alone, unless there is widespread cessation.

But the death tolls of the past need not become the world's future. We know how to control tobacco use. Cessation by the 1.1 billion current smokers is needed to lower tobacco deaths over the next few decades. Reduced uptake of smoking by children would save lives chiefly after 2050. Quitting works: even those who stop smoking in their 40s lower their risk of death remarkably, and those who quit in their 30s have death risks close to lifelong non-smokers.

Tobacco Control Works

Tobacco tax increases, dissemination of information about the health risks of smoking, smoking bans in public, complete bans on advertising and promotion, and cessation therapies are effective in helping smokers to quit. Tobacco taxes are probably the single most cost-effective intervention for adult health in the world. A tripling of the excise tax would roughly double the price of cigarettes (as has happened in New York City), preventing about 3 million deaths per year by 2030.

Most OECD [Organisation for Economic Cooperation and Development, a consortium of 30 countries to which Canada belongs] countries began to take tobacco control seriously in the last two decades, and have decreased male tobacco deaths since. But effective tobacco control measures are not under way in developing countries. Taxes are about 80 percent of the street price of cigarettes in Toronto, but less than 30 percent in Beijing or Delhi. In many countries, tobacco taxes have fallen in real terms. Knowledge of the health risks from smoking is low: 61 percent of Chinese smokers in 1996 thought tobacco did them "little or no harm."

Opposition from the tobacco industry is an obvious obstacle to tobacco control. Spurious economic arguments against higher taxes have been debunked in the West, but are still commonly repeated in the finance ministries of developing countries. Money not spent on tobacco would be spent on other goods and services. Indeed, even sharply reduced demand for tobacco would not mean unemployment in most countries.

Tax hikes lower consumption and raise revenue in the medium-term: a 10 percent higher tax means about 7 percent higher revenue over the medium-term. These funds are a precious resource in fighting poverty. In China, a 10 percent higher price would reduce consumption by 5 percent and raise enough excise revenue to pay for a basic health package for 33 million poor rural Chinese.

Higher Taxes Work

Even in the face of smuggling, higher taxes reduce consumption and raise revenue. Smuggling is abetted by the tobacco

Price Increases Reduce Tobacco Consumption

Evidence from countries of all income levels shows that price increases on cigarettes are highly effective in reducing demand. Higher prices induce cessation and prevent initiation of tobacco use. They also reduce relapse among those who have quit and reduce consumption among continuing users. On average, a 10 percent price increase on a pack of cigarettes would be expected to reduce demand for cigarettes by about 4 percent in high-income countries and by about 8 percent in low- and middle-income countries, where lower incomes tend to make people more sensitive to price changes. Children and adolescents are more sensitive to price increases than adults, allowing price interventions to have a significant impact on this age group.

World Health Organization,
"Tobacco Free Initiative." www.who.int.

industry in order to gain market share and scare finance ministers into lowering taxes. But governments can counter it in several ways: local language warnings with a prominent tax stamp on cigarette packs is one example.

Another common argument against tobacco control—that if people are not harming others, governments should not interfere with their individual decisions—is at odds with both common sense and the evidence.

Most smokers become addicted as adolescents or young adults, when shortsightedness and lack of information make rational decisions difficult. In countries with good information about tobacco risks, by the time child smokers become adults, more than 80 percent wish they never started. Recently, no less a person than [the late conservative journalist] William F. Buckley has argued that nicotine addiction cannot be dismissed as free choice.

Moreover, recent economic research finds that higher taxes are justified on welfare grounds, because the costs to smokers are huge (even though the external costs to others might be small), and that higher cigarette taxes do not hurt the poor (since the self-control value of higher taxes helps the poor more). Nobel laureate Amartya Sen wisely reminds us that "it is important that the practical case for tobacco control is not dismissed on the basis of an incomplete libertarian argument."

The agenda is clear. Governments must take tobacco seriously as a leading killer of adults worldwide. International poverty goals must include tobacco control. Developing countries must not be fooled by the empty economic arguments that paralyzed control efforts in the West for so long. The [Bill and Melinda] Gates Foundation [a major supporter of world health initiatives] can fund action and research. There are hopeful signs: more than 160 countries have signed the World Health Organization's global tobacco control treaty, and the Caribbean heads of state have recently declared they want to tackle tobacco together.

A Reasonable Goal

Between 150 million and 180 million deaths would be avoided before 2050 if the proportion of adults in developing countries who quit smoking increases from below 5 percent today to 30 percent to 40 percent by 2020 (like current quit rates in Canada).

Because control policies deter children from starting, even greater benefits can be expected beyond 2050.

Benjamin Franklin once said: "In this world, nothing can be said to be certain, except death and taxes." Yet we have a tax that could prevent hundreds of millions of premature deaths. It is time to use it.

> *"How convenient for the states that to-bacco is addictive. The states have turned smokers into taxpaying captives, forced now to pay tribute for their nicotine addiction."*

The Government Should Not Tax Tobacco

A.O. Kime

In the following viewpoint, A.O. Kime argues that tobacco taxes and laws regulating tobacco use are unfair because they single out and place an unfair burden on one group of people—smokers. Unequal taxation is unconstitutional, he says, and the states are infringing on the rights of a minority by singling them out for higher taxes. Furthermore, Kime thinks it is clear that health is not the primary reason the states tax tobacco. Instead, he believes tobacco is taxed in order to gather revenues for the states' general funds. In doing this, the states extort the tobacco companies and exploit the addiction of smokers. A.O. Kime lives in Arizona and writes about social issues.

As you read, consider the following questions:

1. According to the author, how much money has the war on drugs cost American taxpayers?

A.O. Kime, "Tobacco Taxation and Constitutional Rights," *Matrix of Mnemosyne*, December 2006. www.matrixbookstore.biz. Reproduced by permission.

2. What reason does the author give for saying that cigarette taxes are "insidiously callous"?

3. Why does the author say it would be a "disaster" for the states if everyone quit smoking?

As if the lessons of Prohibition (alcohol ban) in the 1920's weren't enough, not even America's imbecilic 40-year war on drugs, a war which has cost the American taxpayers an estimated 33 billion dollars with nothing to show for it, unbelievably, smoking is now thought controllable through legislation. Or do the legislators really think tobacco is controllable? Well, that depends on what these 'controls' were intended to do. Were these higher taxes intended to cause people to quit smoking? Not. Was the purpose to raise tax revenue? Absolutely, and the sole purpose. The state's claim that these punishment-style taxes are to encourage people to quit smoking for health reasons has only a smidgen of truth, just enough to become the facade, just like emancipation later became the government's reason for the Civil War. We should know by now, the standard procedure of government is to put a pretty face on everything. . .especially if it's underhanded.

The underhandedness in this case is because it isn't over health concerns at all, as the states claim, but instead it is about raising revenue for the general fund. However, as a result of these high tobacco taxes, the moronic state legislatures have created a sure-to-be constitutional crisis instead. Since unequal taxation is inequitable, it must surely be a human rights violation. . .more specifically an equal rights violation. The higher tax rate on tobacco is inequitable because it doesn't affect all citizens equally, only smokers. It is an attack on a minority group and the legislatures have made it distinguishably an inequitable act. To insure equitability, all products on the market should be taxed at the same rate. It is a constitutional issue. Further, the cost to police any state regulation should always come out of the general fund, not [be] funded by special taxes. . .after all, the whole of society benefits from the totality of laws so the cost to administer them should be equally shared. Importantly, it would help guard against future laws and regulations [that would be] otherwise discriminatory.

For centuries everyone has known smoking isn't a healthy habit. . .but [it is] for many an enjoyable and relaxing habit. While it wouldn't be advisable for anyone to pick up the habit because of the cancer risk, it is only a risk. . .although a greater risk for some than others. Without taking some risks, however, life wouldn't be worth living. . .just ask a skydiver, stunt pilot or mountain climber. Further, in the opinion of many lifelong smokers, it doesn't make a whole lot of sense to quit-. . .going to die from something anyway. It might be from choking on a piece of chicken. . .yet there are no plans to outlaw eating chicken.

So, if not to die of lung cancer, can the states guarantee we will die from something less horrid? In light of these tobacco controls, it seems a guarantee should come with the territory. Well, that was a rhetorical question because tobacco taxes have nothing to do with the government's wish to prolong life. . .it is all about generating revenue for the state coffers. Thanks to smokers now, general services for non-smokers won't cost so much. While smoking can cause cancer in some people, or otherwise reduce a smoker's lifespan a few years, there is a myriad of other potentially deadly hazards. Automobile accidents kill about 50,000 people a year but no one dare say it's better than dying from lung cancer. One can't say being burned alive would be better either.

Besides tobacco taxation being insidiously callous because it targets an addiction, the same as if to overtax a diabetic's insulin, there are seven (7) reasons listed below why the smokers tax is either criminal, unjust, unhealthy and economically detrimental:

1. States Have Conspired to Extort the Tobacco Companies

When the states finally began winning in court against the tobacco giants about seven years ago, . . .while the monetary awards were legally obtained, nonetheless they were fraudulently obtained. Through their use of advocacy science [science used to further a political agenda] the states committed wholesale perjury. Effectively, it was also extortion.

Aside from fraud and extortion, there exist other horrid realities. While the complaint was that the states had been bearing the cost to treat smoking related illnesses, and true to some minuscule degree, only the reimbursement for direct aid is justifiably due the states. The monies awarded the states were also intended to provide them with funds necessary to treat future patients. While that would appear reasonable and fair, but of what little tobacco revenue does go towards their so-called 'tobacco prevention programs', the states are spending it on salaries and the printing press. Counseling smokers and inundating them with brochures on how to quit smoking doesn't do someone suffering from lung cancer much good. There is little, if any, direct aid to smokers to help defray medical costs. While counseling and brochures might seem a good way to help people kick the habit and help keep kids from smoking in the first place, incredibly most states have recently slashed even these programs despite a bonanza of additional tobacco tax revenue. . . .

Even though the tobacco companies shouldn't be held liable for smoker illnesses, largely due to the fact everyone has known for centuries smoking wasn't healthy . . . , but if a smoker did have a legitimate claim, then he (or she) [should be] entitled to compensation, not the states. Nor are the states passing it on. A similar circumstance would be if the states were awarded the death benefits from everyone's life insurance policy.

From the tobacco settlement to the endless tax increases on tobacco, the entire matter is the cruelest and the most insidious undertaking America has witnessed since Prohibition. It not only reeks of greed and callousness, it is the embodiment of pure underhandedness.

2. States Are Using the Funds Intended for Treating Smoking Illnesses for Other Purposes

Not only was perjury committed in obtaining these victories and the amount collected...much more than...actual out-of-pocket costs, most states are using the funds intended for treating smoking illnesses for other purposes....

3. States Are Infringing on Human Rights by Singling a Minority for Higher Taxes

Flush with victory over the tobacco companies, the states then began another attack, this time on the smokers themselves by increasing taxes on tobacco to a punishing degree. It has reached a point whereby smoking has become a big-ticket item for most smokers, now a substantial portion of their household budget. The states contend that they raised taxes to discourage smoking but that is only the stated purpose...the real reason is to increase tax revenue to support their ever-increasing bloated budgets. It would be a disaster for the states if everyone quit smoking...but many smokers can't because it is addictive.

4. The Resulting Black Market and Cheap Roll-Your-Own Cigarettes Pose a Greater Health Risk

What were the legislators thinking? A black market would be inevitable and, as prohibition and the current drug war has confirmed, substance abuse cannot be legislated away. As a result, both untaxed and counterfeit cigarettes are now for sale in the growing black market. Since it has been reported that it only costs $2.00 a carton for counterfeiters to produce, the quality of the tobacco comes into question. Furthermore, with the cost per pack so high many smokers are resorting to rolling their own and most often smoke them without filters. . .creating a greater risk to one's health. In the end, the states took a 'potential' health hazard and made it worse.

5. Cost of Smoking Is Hurting Other Businesses

The cost of smoking has become a big-ticket item for most smokers, spending now $100–$150 per month for cigarettes (per smoker). . .taking a huge bite out of their budgeted amount for incidentals. For each dollar spent on cigarette taxes is a dollar being denied other businesses. . . less to be spent on entertainment, eating out and for other such nonessentials. For another pack of cigarettes, most smokers will forgo a new pair of pants or a knickknack they'd like to have. The amount a state has taken out of circulation is easy to calculate . . .it is whatever that state's tobacco tax revenue is, averaging $400 million annually per state. For all 50 states, an incredible $20 billion per year is being collected annually.

6. Smoking Regulations Imposed on Private Businesses Are Attacks on Property Rights

Mandating private businesses to provide a smoke-free environment, aside from violating the owner's property rights, is an act which interferes with supply and demand, the basis of a free marketplace. If it affects a business in a negative way, then that in itself signals it isn't what the majority of their customers wanted. If having a smoke-free environment was truly the public sentiment, business owners would have rushed to fill the need. But it isn't the public sentiment as the states claim. Further, the health risks from secondhand smoke, if any, cannot logically be made a health issue of great concern while the exhaust fumes from traffic are far worse. A dust storm and household aerosols are worse. These studies indicating otherwise cannot be trusted. . .after all, who sponsored them?. . .Secondhand smoke is assuredly the least dangerous of all air contaminates.

7. States Are Taking Advantage of the Addiction to Tobacco

How convenient for the states that tobacco is addictive. The states have turned smokers into taxpaying captives, forced now to pay tribute for their nicotine addiction. For that reason it is a very cruel tax. If cruelty is to exist, then cruelty should be evenhanded. . .equally over-taxed then should be insulin, pacemakers and exercise machines. The states can claim some evenhandedness however. . .such as keeping the cost for health-care out of reach for almost everyone. A just tyrant, after all, is better than just a tyrant.

Tyranny for All

Unequal taxation amounts to subjugation, and in the smoker's case. . .callous subjugation. It is clear, the states have abandoned all notions of protecting the rights of its citizens. . .only the pretext of protection remains. Health is not the issue in the state's war on tobacco. . .the states don't give a damn about health. . .zero, nada, zilch. If they did they'd be forking out their tobacco revenue on actual treatments. Further, most of the states have actually cut their tobacco prevention programs and in many states as much as 75% of tobacco revenue goes into their general fund. The remaining 25% is spent mainly on administrating nothingness and thus serves their empire-building agenda more than ill-affected smokers. Of little substance, these programs are empty shells with a facade psychologically engineered to reflect otherwise.

The insurance companies, as co-beneficiaries, have gained as well but they won't be happy until tobacco is outlawed. In that the state legislatures continue to placate them is simply outrageous. Insurance companies are the scourge of modern-day society as they continually cause the usurpation of human rights through bribery (campaign contributions) to serve their own interests.

The conduct of the states is alarming, disgusting and even treasonous. In addition, to attack smoking but let alone alcohol is absurd and the height of hypocrisy. Comparatively, alcohol is 10 times worse. . .far worse even than marijuana or cocaine. If 'sins' are to be attacked, they should be attacked in order of the danger they pose. To attack only the lesser sins, and to leave the greater ones standing unchallenged, is totally hypocritical and this hypocritical posture is the main reason for substance abuse in the first place.

Setting Things Right

Perhaps some relief is in sight however. Every so often the federal government will step in to correct human rights violations by the states. . .like what the Civil Rights Act of 1964 [the major piece of legislation outlawing discrimination based on race, religion, ethnicity, and gender] did. This is another such time the situation calls for it. There are some provisions within this same Civil Rights Act which would apply. . .and, fortunately, federal intervention is allowed in these instances as provided for in the 14th Amendment [containing "Due Process" and "Equal Protection" clauses, this post-Civil War amendment to the U.S. Constitution is a linchpin of antidiscrimination laws]. Further, the 1948 [United Nations] Universal Declaration of Human Rights applies.

When the day comes [that] the United States Supreme Court rules these tobacco taxes unconstitutional, the perpetrators, the legislators who voted for this mess, should be imprisoned. After all, without lawmakers being held accountable they'll continually try sneaking something unconstitutional into law. The states should also be forced to reimburse smokers. . .even if it bankrupts the state, and it will. . .it would be a great lesson for the states.

So to hell with state's rights. . .["state's rights" is a term that is sometimes used to refer to Southern opposition to Civil-Rights legislation] the states are proving themselves completely hostile to the idea of protecting human rights. They've gotten so bad the feds now look like choir boys. While once sympathetic to the Southern Cause and state's rights, often wishing the South had won (the Civil War), now I'm glad they didn't. No more gray for me. . .except after buying cigarettes today, I ain't got no money left to buy blue clothes. Sorry mister and missus merchant. . .all my extra money went to the state treasury.

> "A few years ago it would have been un-imaginable that Virginia's State Senate would vote to ban smoking in bars, restaurants and other public places. . . . Americans are losing their tolerance for what once was a symbol of their culture."

Most Americans Believe Smoking Should Be Banned in Public Places

Stephen Kaufman

In the following viewpoint, Stephen Kaufman asserts that the American public has changed its attitude toward smoking. Eleven states have banned smoking in indoor public places such as bars and restaurants, and surveys show that 39 percent of Americans now live in areas covered by such bans. Kaufman supports his assertion that public attitudes are changing in an interview with John F. Banzhaf, an attorney who teaches public interest law at George Washington Law School in Washington, D.C. Smoking bans are widely seen as an effort to protect the health of non-smokers. Stephen Kaufman is a staff writer for the Washington File, *published by the U.S. Department of State.*

Stephen Kaufman, "Americans Increasingly Opposed to Smoking in Public Places," United States Embassy, Montevideo, Uruguay, February 21, 2006. http://monte video.usembassy.gov. Reproduced by permission.

As you read, consider the following questions:

1. When did efforts to ban smoking first begin to appear, and why?

2. How does John F. Banzhaf define a "smoke-free society"?

3. What factors, according to Banzhaf, are driving down the number of teen smokers?

Only a few years ago it would have been unimaginable that Virginia's State Senate would vote to ban smoking in bars, restaurants and other public places. But [recently], in the U.S. state whose history and economy have been so closely tied to tobacco, and where tobacco industry giant Philip Morris is based, lawmakers in Richmond provided the latest evidence that Americans are losing their tolerance for what once was a symbol of their culture.

Although the measure is not expected to pass Virginia's House of Delegates, 11 U.S. states have enacted laws banning smoking in indoor public places, including bars and restaurants. The group Americans for Nonsmokers' Rights reported at the end of 2005 that 39 percent of U.S. citizens now live in areas that "are covered by statewide or local laws limiting smoking."

The issue, according to many anti-smoking activists, is not a desire to curtail the freedom of smokers, but rather to protect the health of nonsmokers.

The Culture Has Changed

Gone are Joe Camel and the Marlboro Man from their former prevalence on U.S. billboards, replaced by anti-smoking ads under terms of the 1999 tobacco settlement [in which tobacco companies agreed to pay 46 states $206 billion in damages]. And smoking has been forbidden on all domestic U.S. flights, and the majority of flights to and from the United States, because of efforts on the part of groups like Action on Smoking and Health (ASH), founded by professor John F. Banzhaf, who teaches and practices public interest law at the George Washington University Law School in Washington.

In an interview with the *Washington File*, Banzhaf said it is without question that the American public has changed its attitude toward smoking and tobacco.

"We are much less tolerant toward smoking. We are much more willing to ban smoking and to go far further than we would have only a few years ago," he said.

Efforts to ban smoking have been developing since the early 1990s when research showed that secondhand smoke not only was an annoyance to nonsmokers, but actually was contributing to their deaths from lung cancer. Banzhaf said it now is also known that exposure to secondhand smoke can trigger a heart attack.

He said ASH serves as "the major nonsmokers rights organization in the United States" and as "a catalyst to bring and encourage legal and law-related actions to protect the rights of nonsmokers."

Building on Successes

Having achieved success in prohibiting smoking in many indoor public areas in several states and localities, ASH now also is targeting outdoor smoking in public places on the grounds that tobacco smoke is a "toxic air contaminant" along the lines of dangerous automotive and industrial air pollutants.

On January 26 [2006], the California Air Resources Board formally declared outdoor tobacco smoke to be a toxic air contaminant, an action which Banzhaf said would "trigger a complex legal mechanism. . .result[ing] in a lot more bans on smoking outdoors." Indeed, the city of Calabasas, California, passed a comprehensive secondhand smoke control ordinance on February 15 [2006] that bans smoking virtually everywhere outdoors, including sidewalks, streets, restaurant patios and parking lots.

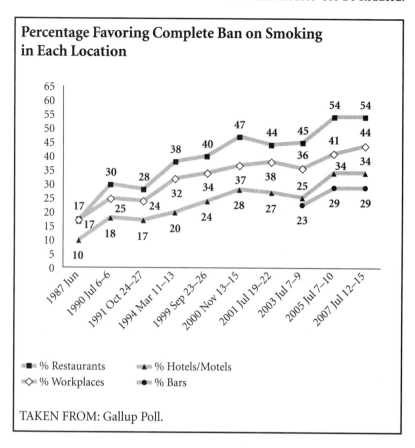

Percentage Favoring Complete Ban on Smoking in Each Location

% Restaurants   % Hotels/Motels
% Workplaces   % Bars

TAKEN FROM: Gallup Poll.

"The only place smoking is going to be permitted is what they call a few small 'smokers' outposts," he said, referring to small, well-marked areas that will be provided to smokers in some shopping malls.

Banzhaf said that within the next few years the majority of U.S. states will be "totally smoke-free indoors," with perhaps one or two that also have banned outdoor smoking, and speculated that the momentum would continue.

"The ultimate goal is to have a smoke-free society, by which we don't mean that nobody will smoke, but it will be something like spitting which is not done politely in public," he said. "We will not be tolerating it on public places, streets, outdoors or anywhere else."

Smoking Bans Discourage New Smokers

The smoking bans, in addition to protecting the health of nonsmokers, also are discouraging many young people from taking up the habit, as well as influencing others to give it up.

The bans "are not only making it more inconvenient to be a smoker, but they turn the smoking message on its head," he said.

"We used to get the message from everybody from James Bond to the ads that smoking made you sexy and sociable and sophisticated. Today all those no-smoking sections and no-smoking signs are sending just the opposite message to the kids. Smoking makes you stinky and smelly, not sociable. That combined with higher taxes is what is driving down teen consumption," he said.

As the number of adult smokers in the United States continues to fall, Banzhaf says popular influence and pressure on local city and state governments to enact smoking bans is now "the major factor" in the goal of achieving a smoke-free society.

| "Forty-five million adults in the U.S.—
| about 21 percent of the population—
| choose to smoke. . . . You cannot simply
| run rough-shod over their rights."

Smoking Should Not Be Banned in Public Places

Joseph Bast

In the following viewpoint, Joseph Bast argues that "people are free to do things both great and foolish so long as they do not conflict with an equal right held by others." This includes smoking. Since scientific studies have not conclusively established the harmfulness of secondhand smoke, smoking bans should not be established in law, he says. There is evidence that fewer people are smoking, even in places where laws have not been passed, and he believes that individual freedoms should be preserved. Joseph Bast is president and CEO of the Heartland Institute, a nonprofit research and educational organization that promotes free market solutions to social and economic problems.

As you read, consider the following questions:

1. According to John Stuart Mill, whom Bast quotes in this viewpoint, is it acceptable to exercise power over other people in order to protect them from their own actions?

Joseph Bast, "Leave Those Poor Smokers Alone!" The Heartland Institute, January 1, 2006. www.heartland.org. Reproduced by permission.

2. What are some of the reasons why Bast is critical of the anti-smoking movement?

3. Why are cigarette taxes unfair, according to Bast?

A member of the Heartland Institute's board of directors called me recently to ask why I spend time defending smokers. It's a lost cause, he said, and it surely doesn't win us any friends.

I know smoking is widely condemned and that banning smoking in restaurants and bars is all the rage among state and local elected officials. I know many people think they unfairly shoulder the higher health costs of smokers, hate tobacco companies, and can't stand the smell of cigarettes. And I know my writing on this subject will irk some Heartland supporters.

I know all that. . .but I still think it is important to defend smokers. Here are my reasons.

Smokers Have Rights

Forty-five million adults in the U.S.—about 21 percent of the population—choose to smoke. You probably know a few who do. You can detest their habit and support regulations that protect you from any adverse effects their smoking may have on you, but you cannot simply run rough-shod over their rights. They're still people. They still have rights.

[Philosopher] John Stuart Mill wrote in 1859, "The only purpose for which power can be rightfully exercised over any member of a civilized community against his will is to prevent harm to others. His own good, either physical or moral, is not a sufficient warrant."

We live in a nation founded on that principle. People are free to do things both great and foolish so long as they do not conflict with an equal right held by others. That focus on individual liberty is the reason we are the most prosperous and tolerant people in human history. When we carve out exceptions to this principle, we ought to do so with great care and reluctance.

I see neither great care nor reluctance in the anti-smoking movement. Instead I see a $600 million-a-year anti-smoking industry, funded largely by taxes on tobacco products, willing to use junk science, scare tactics, lawsuit abuse, and government force to demonize a product and its users. It's a textbook campaign for stealing the rights of a minority and making government bigger and more powerful. It should be repugnant to anyone who is a friend of freedom.

Smokers Pay for Their Habit

When calculating the "costs of smoking" it is important to remember that smokers assume the risk, which means they understand the risk to their health but decide that risk is worth taking for the enjoyment they derive from smoking. Whatever losses smokers themselves sustain are not "costs to society" that justify higher taxes or restrictions on smoking.

The 2004 average retail price of a pack of cigarettes was $3.82. The federal tax was $0.47, state tax $1.41...nearly half the retail price. Smokers in some states pay more in taxes on cigarettes than in state income taxes, which is a polite way of saying smokers are forced to pay twice as much in state taxes as nonsmokers.

[Former] Harvard University professor Kip Viscusi has repeatedly demonstrated that smokers paid more in excise taxes than the social costs of their habits even before the 1999 Master Settlement Agreement [in which tobacco companies agreed to reimburse 46 states for harm caused by their products] raised the price of a pack of cigarettes by $0.40. (All that money goes directly into state government coffers and is spent largely for the benefit of nonsmokers.) Says Viscusi, "excise taxes on cigarettes equal or exceed the medical care costs associated with smoking."

A Deeply Rooted Problem

If tobacco cigarettes were now being introduced into the marketplace for the first time, there is no doubt that they would be banned under any one of several consumer protection statutes. Of course, banning tobacco products is not feasible or wise. The challenge the country faces today is to develop a feasible strategy for rooting out a problem that is deeply entrenched in our economic and cultural life. There are still 45 million cigarette smokers and another 9.7 million users of other tobacco products. Most of them regret taking up the habit and struggle to quit.

Richard Bonnie, "Ending the Tobacco Problem,"
The Institute of Medicine, May 24, 2007.

That was back in 2001. . .before the enormous hikes in cigarette taxes of recent years. It also doesn't take into account the politically incorrect but nevertheless undeniable fact that smokers save the rest of society by qualifying for fewer years of Social Security and private pension benefits. Smokers die, on average, six to seven years before nonsmokers.

Arguments Based on Junk Science

The only legitimate grounds for interfering in smokers' choices are the potentially harmful effects of second-hand smoke on nonsmokers. Anti-smoking activists say second-hand smoke contains 4,000 poisons and carcinogens, that even a tiny dose can cause severe health effects. They claim "there is no safe level of exposure to second-hand smoke."

This is pure junk science. The first principle of toxicology is that the dose makes the poison. We are exposed to thousands of natural poisons and carcinogens in our diets every day, but they don't hurt us because the exposure is too small to overcome our bodies' natural defenses. The same is true of second-hand smoke. No victim of cancer, heart disease, etc. can "prove" his or her cancer or heart disease was caused by exposure to second-hand smoke.

Perhaps the best recent academic study of the effects of second-smoke on nonsmokers appeared in a 2003 issue of the *British Medical Journal*. The authors analyzed data collected by the American Cancer Society from more than 100,000 Californians from 1959 through 1997. They concluded: "The results do not support a causal relation between environmental tobacco smoke and tobacco-related mortality," although they do not rule out a small effect. "The association between tobacco smoke and coronary heart disease and lung cancer may be considerably weaker than generally believed."

Various radical environmental groups and liberal advocacy groups have been warning us about the supposed risk of "getting cancer" from everything from apples and soda to coffee, chocolate, french fries, and fish. . .and now second-hand smoke. Yet each year Americans are living longer and healthier lives. Cancer rates are going down, not up. Do the math, guys.

Coercion Is Not Necessary

We don't need more bans on smoking in public spaces because people are figuring this out on their own. In the first place, fewer people are smoking. Controlling for the tar content of cigarettes, per-capita cigarette consumption fell by three-fifths (60 percent) since 1950, according to Viscusi.

In most cities and towns, more than half the restaurants are already nonsmoking by choice, and virtually every restaurant has seats reserved for nonsmokers. A growing share have physical room dividers and ventilation systems to prevent smoke migration. Few smokers who share a home with a nonsmoker smoke indoors anymore, or at least not in rooms likely to be occupied by nonsmoking family members.

All this is working. Exposure to second-hand smoke, as measured by the amount of cotinine [a metabolite of nicotine] in the blood of nonsmokers, has fallen 68 percent for kids and 75 percent for adults from the four-year period 1988–1991 to the four-year period 1999–2002, according to the Centers for Disease Control.

Recall that even exposure to much higher levels of second-hand smoke in the past hasn't been plausibly associated with negative health effects. . .so how likely is it that today's much lower levels of exposure are a real public health threat? Not very.

Freedoms Must Be Protected

So let's see. Taxes are already far above any reasonable estimate of social costs of smoking, sound science doesn't show a health risk from second-hand smoke, voluntary limits now make smoke-free restaurants and even bars widely available to nonsmokers, and exposure to second-hand smoke is rapidly diminishing. Gee, what should we do?

[Economist and philosopher] Friedrich Hayek once wrote, "if we wish to preserve a free society, it is essential that we recognize that the desirability of a particular object is not sufficient justification for the use of coercion." Surely this is a case where further coercion is not justified.

Anti-smoking lobbyists want to go one step further by banning smoking in the few places left for smokers to go to enjoy their habits: those restaurants and bars whose owners still permit smoking. I don't blame them for wanting to do this because continuing to attack smokers is their business, and I mean that literally: They are paid to advocate smoking restrictions.

I'm not paid to defend smokers. Heartland probably loses funding every time I write on this subject. But as I see it, somebody has to stand up for the millions of American smokers who just want to be left alone. Enough already! Leave those poor smokers alone!

> *"The best way to prevent the problems that can develop due to smoking is to prevent children from ever smoking in the first place."*

Smoking Prevention Efforts Should Focus on Children

Leann M. Lesperance and Henry H. Bernstein

In the following viewpoint, Leann M. Lesperance and Henry H. Bernstein argue that smoking prevention should begin in childhood. Parents who smoke should quit, they say, in order to set a good example for their children. In addition, they believe parents should talk to their children at a very young age about the unpleasant and unhealthy consequences of smoking. Teens who have already started smoking need clear messages and support from parents, as well as a good example, to help them break the habit before it becomes more serious. They recommend that parents who do continue to smoke take steps to limit their children's exposure to secondhand smoke. Leann M. Lesperance and Henry H. Bernstein are physicians at Boston Children's Hospital.

As you read, consider the following questions:

1. What are some of the many smoking-related symptoms and illnesses named by the authors?

2. How do the authors suggest that a parent should respond to a teenager who has started to smoke?

3. According to the authors, can air-cleaning machines remove dangerous smoke-related particles from the air?

The Great American Smokeout is held each year on the third Thursday of November to encourage smokers to quit. In addition, all parents can use this event to start talking about the dangers of tobacco with their children.

Tobacco use is currently the single most preventable cause of death in the United States. People who start smoking early in life have the highest risk of smoking-related symptoms and illnesses including coughing, shortness of breath, colds, sinus infections, lung infections (pneumonia), lung cancer, poor physical fitness, heart disease and overall poorer health. Adolescents who smoke are more likely to use alcohol and illegal drugs, carry weapons, attempt suicide and engage in high-risk sexual behaviors.

The best way to prevent the problems that can develop due to smoking is to prevent children from ever smoking in the first place. When children and adolescents smoke, this often starts a lifelong smoking pattern. It is very easy for children and adolescents to become addicted to nicotine. An adolescent who completes high school without ever smoking is very unlikely to become a smoker in adulthood.

To prevent smoking in children, it is important for all parents to talk with their children about tobacco, starting at an early age. Here are some suggestions for getting the important messages about tobacco across to your children:

- Explain that smoking is extremely dangerous and very unhealthy. It definitely causes trouble breathing and makes it harder to run and play sports.

- Point out that tobacco smoke smells bad, stains teeth, fingernails and skin, and even makes clothes, hair and breath smell bad, too.

- Remind your child that most young people do *not* smoke or chew tobacco. Children see many cigarette ads and references to smoking in the media and may think that smoking is more common than it truly is.

- Role play with your child to prepare him for dealing with pressure from friends to try tobacco. Pretend to be a classmate or friend offering your child a cigarette and let your child practice different responses.

- When you see cigarette ads, talk with your child about what the ads are actually trying to sell: maturity, beauty, sexual attraction, wealth and "coolness." Make it clear that cigarette smoking cannot provide anybody with these things.

If your child or adolescent begins smoking, try the following suggestions, adapted from the U.S. Centers for Disease Control and Prevention (CDC):

- If *you* smoke, try to quit. If you did smoke and have already quit, talk to your child about your experience. Talk about the challenges you faced when trying to quit. Teens and preteens often believe they can quit smoking whenever they want, but research shows many teens never do.

- Ask what changes can be made in your child's life to help her stop smoking.

- Avoid threats and ultimatums. Ask a few questions and find out why your child feels the need to smoke. Your child may want to be accepted by his peers or may be looking for attention. We also know how stressful adolescence can be—your child could be smoking to relieve stress. If so, try to help your child lower their stress level and find another outlet for it.

- Be supportive. Both you and your teen need to be ready for the mood swings and crankiness that can come with nicotine withdrawal when someone tries to stop smoking. Offer your teen the Five Ds to get through the tough times:

- *Delay*—The craving will eventually go away.

- *Deep breathe*—Take a few calming deep breaths.

- *Drink water*—It helps cool the oral desire for a cigarette.

- *Do something else*—Find a new habit.

- *Discuss*—Talk about your thoughts and feelings.

- Have your teen or preteen write down all the reasons why she wants to quit. Refer back to this list when your teen is tempted.

- Finally, reward your teen when she quits. Plan something special to do together.

If you smoke, plan to quit today! You can use the Five Ds to help. Don't forget that exposure to secondhand smoke is also a significant health issue for children. Some of the harmful chemicals in secondhand smoke include nicotine, carbon monoxide and benzene. Exposure to passive smoke has been associated with ear infections, chronic breathing [problems] and infections, and poor lung function. Childhood exposure to smoke may increase the risk of developing environmental allergies and asthma, and can increase the number of emergency-room visits made by children who have asthma. Children of smokers also have more than three times the risk

Secondhand Smoke Threatens Children's Health

Making your home smoke-free may be one of the most important things you can do for the health of your family. Any family member can develop health problems related to secondhand smoke. Children are especially sensitive. In the United States, 21 million, or 35% of children live in homes where residents or visitors smoke in the home on a regular basis. About 50% to 75% of children in the United States have detectable levels of cotinine, the breakdown product of nicotine, in their blood.

American Cancer Society. www.cancer.org.

of sudden infant death syndrome (SIDS) than children of nonsmokers, and risk is increased with number of cigarettes smoked per day.

If you cannot yet quit, keep the dangers to a minimum by limiting as much of your children's exposure to tobacco as possible. Smoke outside, and *never* smoke in the car. If you smoke in the house, use a room with good ventilation. Air-cleaning machines do not remove all the dangerous particles from the air. . . .Remember that one of the best gifts you can give your children is keeping the air clean around them.

> *"The focus on children reflects the imperative of fashioning restrictive measures to avoid the charge that adults are being told what to do for their own good."*

It Could Be a Mistake to Focus Smoking Prevention Efforts on Children

Ronald Bayer and Valeri Kiesig

In the following viewpoint, Ronald Bayer and Valeri Kiesig argue that tobacco prevention efforts need to focus on adult smokers, who are most at risk of serious illness and death. Historically, they say, tobacco and smoking prevention in the United States has focused on children, because of the influence of American individualism, which limits the ability to fashion public health policy aimed at the dangerous behaviors of adults. The authors make the case that in order to significantly reduce the harm caused by tobacco, public health policy must focus on the behaviors of adults. Ronald Bayer and Valeri Kiesig are with the Mailman School of Public Health at Columbia University, New York.

Ronald Bayer and Valeri Kiesig, "Is Child-Centered Tobacco Prevention a Trap?" *American Journal of Public Health*, March 2003. www.pubmedcentral.nih.gov. Reproduced by permission.

As you read, consider the following questions:

1. What are some of the ways the tobacco industry has encouraged young children and adolescents to smoke, according to Bayer and Kiesig?

2. What do the authors mean when they say "the core of parental and governmental concern has subtly shifted weight from the moral to the medical"?

3. According to the authors, how does addiction interfere with an individual's freedom to choose to smoke or not to smoke?

"There is no question that demands more public attention...than the prevailing methods of cigarette manufacturers to foster and stimulate smoking among children," an angry New Yorker said in 1888. Tobacco manufacturers seduced the young with promotional prizes like pocket knives and lithograph albums, he said. "At the office of a leading factory in this city you can see any Saturday afternoon a crowd of children with vouchers clamoring for the reward of self-inflicted injury."

More than a century later, David Kessler, then Food and Drug Administration Commissioner, held a private meeting with President Clinton. Kessler described a similar scene: Adolescents lured by the T-shirts and hats they could buy with Camel cash or Marlboro miles, 6-year-olds taken in by the fun cartoon character Joe Camel, and underage smokers finding easy access to cigarettes in vending machines, in self-service displays, and from lax store clerks. "They all think they can quit," Kessler said, "but then nicotine hooks them." Smoking as he described it was no longer the fault of the young smoker but a "pediatric disease" propagated by the tobacco industry. Kessler said that the president was angry. Clinton reportedly said of those responsible in the tobacco companies, "I want to kill them."

The Goals of Prevention Have Changed

The instinct to protect children that was present in both the 1880s and the 1990s reflects the central obligation public health has always had to the young and vulnerable. In 1888, though, parents worried largely about the social disease of smoking, how cigarettes might stain childhood purity. Today the desire is to protect children from the disease of addiction, which might lead to grave medical consequences in adulthood. The core of parental and governmental concern has subtly shifted weight from the moral to the medical. Children still garner ethical concerns but not, as in the past, because cigarettes will weaken their character. Instead, the call to protect children is framed by the growing number of tobacco-related deaths. Of course it is not children who are dying. Rather it is the nicotine-addicted adults these children are likely to become.

The moral challenge posed by tobacco use and nicotine addiction in children was stated pointedly by philosopher Robert Goodin: "Being below the age of consent when they first began smoking, smokers were incapable of meaningfully consenting to the risks in the first instance. Being addicted by the time they reached the age of consent, they were incapable of consenting later either."

The focus on children and adolescents was also an outgrowth of the epidemiological challenge posed by tens of millions of *adult* smokers. The 1994 surgeon general's report *Preventing Tobacco Use Among Young People* was bold in its assertion: "When young people no longer want to smoke the epidemic itself will die." Echoing this perspective the Institute of Medicine declared in the same year, "In the long run tobacco use can be most efficiently reduced through a policy aimed at preventing children and adolescents from initiating tobacco use."

It was this framing of the issue that informed much of the debate in the 1990s on advertising restrictions and on the imposition of ever-stiffer excise taxes on cigarettes.

Framing the Issue in Different Terms

When in 1996 the Food and Drug Administration proposed its Supreme Court–thwarted final rule on nicotine, the limits on [cigarette] advertising were solely focused on the protection of those younger than 18 years. [In 1996 the FDA claimed regulatory jurisdiction over tobacco, including the power to regulate advertising. Their proposed new tobacco policy was called the Final Rule. This was later challenged and struck down in the U.S. Supreme Court. See Preface to Chapter 3 for more on the Final Rule.] [The FDA's] counteradvertising proposals were justified as a way of undoing "the effects of the pervasive advertising that for decades has influenced young people to begin and continue using tobacco products." Such restrictions would "preserve the component of advertising and labeling which can provide product information to adult smokers" despite the inevitable impact on what adults would be able to see. And when Massachusetts sought to implement severe advertising restrictions that were ultimately overturned by the Supreme Court, it did so in the name of protecting children.

With cigarette taxes, too, the emphasis on child protection can be seen. When efforts to raise such levies were explicit about their potential public health benefits, the argument in the late 1980s and early 1990s was almost always about making it more difficult for adolescents, with limited disposable income, to buy cigarettes. In Massachusetts, for example, the proponents of a 1992 referendum to impose a 25-cent tax on each pack of cigarettes stated: "We are not after an adult habit—we're after keeping kids from smoking. . . .Once kids are addicted they're trapped for life."

The Difference Age Makes

To our knowledge, the present study is the first to date to examine smoking cessation program participation among young adult smokers. . . .

Those young adult smokers who were older were more likely to participate in the smoking cessation program compared with younger smokers. Although, the smoking history and smoking habits of young adult smokers have received little attention, one could speculate that young adults in their mid-twenties are more serious about quitting than young adult smokers 18 to 20 years old. As young adult smokers progress through their twenties, graduate college, and/or obtain a job (i.e., acquire more adult roles), quit attempts may become more serious and translate into successful cessation.

Janet Audrain McGovern, et al.,
"Predictors of Participation in a Smoking
Cessation Program Among Young Adult Smokers,"
Cancer Epidemiology Biomarkers and Prevention,
March 1, 2007.

Paternalism and Individualism in Conflict

What can account for the emphasis placed on children in the campaign against tobacco? Certainly those who have devoted themselves to confronting the awful human burden caused by cigarette smoking believe that they can "save" children and the adults they will become by interrupting the uptake of tobacco use. But more is at stake. Just as the emphasis on the innocent victims of environmental tobacco smoke reflects the need to fashion policies that can avoid the taint of paternalism, the focus on children reflects the imperative of fashioning restrictive measures to avoid the charge that adults are being told what to do for their own good. Thus the focus on children demonstrates the constraining influence of American individualism on public health policy.

But what if the focus on children not only represents an ideological dead end but will miss the public health mark that justifies such measures? It may be true that those who begin to smoke as adolescents continue to smoke into their adult years. It may not follow, however, that those who do not smoke as adolescents do not smoke as adults. What if it is untrue that smoking prevented in adolescence is smoking averted?...It may, in the end, be necessary to say clearly that a public health campaign that does not give great emphasis to limiting adult smoking is doomed.

Periodical Bibliography

The following articles have been selected to supplement the diverse views presented in this chapter.

Chemist & Druggist	"Pharmacy Update: Helping the Nicotine Pariahs," March 3, 2007.
Myra Dembrow	"How to Help Patients Stop the Smoking Habit: Chewing Tobacco Should Not Be an Alternative, New Research Confirms," *Clinical Advisor*, January 2008.
Liz French	"An Ounce of Prevention: Cheryl Healton Explains How This Public Health Organization Is Helping Youth Say No to Tobacco," *American Executive*, July 2007.
Chee Gates	"O's Smoking Challenge: You Couldn't Find a Smarter, Nicer, Kinder Bunch Than the Women in Our Online Stop-Smoking Support Group," *O, The Oprah Magazine*, January 2007.
Noreena Hertz	"How to Stand Up to Big Tobacco," *New Statesman*, June 12, 2006.
Brian Hindo	"An Antismoking 'Call to Action': A New World Health Organization Study Calls for Regulation, Education, and Taxation to Combat Rising Smoking Rates in the Developing World," *Business Week Online*, Feb 8, 2008.
Jane Salodof MacNeil	"Vaccine May Help Some Heavy Smokers to Quit," *Internal Medicine News*, November 1, 2005.
Marshall Tanick	"Commentary: Smoking Bans in the Workplace Raise Burning Legal Issues," *Daily Record* (Kansas City, MO), March 9, 2005.
Update	"Smoking Cessation: A Rational Approach," January 2007.

OPPOSING
VIEWPOINTS®
SERIES

CHAPTER 3

Should the Food and Drug Administration Regulate Tobacco?

Chapter Preface

In 1996, the U.S. Food and Drug Administration (FDA) published the "FDA Rule," asserting its authority to regulate tobacco under the Food, Drug, and Cosmetic Act, and laying out a regulatory framework for federal tobacco control policy. The regulations issued by the FDA at that time established legal guidelines for advertising and marketing campaigns; set strict standards for labeling tobacco products; and placed restrictions on the purchase of tobacco by youth. The tobacco industry responded by filing suit against the federal government, arguing that the FDA did not have jurisdiction over tobacco products. It claimed that tobacco products are neither drugs nor drug delivery devices, and it argued that the section of the FDA Rule restricting tobacco marketing violated the industry's freedom of speech, as protected by the First Amendment of the U.S. Constitution. The U.S. Supreme Court eventually found in favor of the tobacco industry. It ruled in March of 2000 that in order for the FDA to regulate the manufacture and sale of tobacco products, Congress would need to enact legislation that specifically designated this as a power of the agency. The Supreme Court's ruling means that most of the federal regulations that governed the marketing and sale of tobacco products in the mid-1990s are no longer enforceable.

According to the American Heart Association, the remaining federal regulations governing the tobacco industry do little to protect U.S. consumers. This is true in spite of the fact that nearly 440,000 Americans die annually from tobacco-related diseases. "Unlike other companies whose products are consumed by humans," the American Heart Association claims, "tobacco companies are not bound by common-sense laws, like the requirement to disclose ingredients and warn about carcinogens. Surgeon General warnings, prohibition of television advertising, and some agricultural safeguards are the only Federal tools left to educate and protect American consumers."

In February of 2007, two bills were introduced in Congress that would address what the American Heart Association and a number of other organizations believe is a legislative vacuum left by the 2000 Supreme Court ruling. In the U.S. House of Representatives, Henry Waxman (D-CA) and Tom Davis (R-VA) sponsored H.R. 1108, while Senators Edward Kennedy (D-MA) and John Cornyn (R-TX) sponsored S. 625. The House and Senate bills together are known as the Family Smoking Prevention and Tobacco Control Act.

The new legislation would reinstate the 1996 FDA Rule on youth access and marketing. Specifically, it would ban outdoor advertising within 1,000 feet of schools and playgrounds, ban tobacco brand sponsorship of sports and entertainment events, ban gift-with-purchase programs in connection with tobacco sales, as well as a number of other measures aimed at reducing youth access to tobacco products. It would also grant the FDA authority to impose future restrictions on tobacco marketing practices without congressional approval. The bill would empower the FDA to evaluate the content of tobacco products and to require product modifications in order to protect the public health, and it would affirm the rights of individual states to pass their own tobacco control laws.

The Family Smoking Prevention and Tobacco Control Act is supported by many in the public health community, including the American Cancer Society, the American Lung Association, and the Campaign for Tobacco-Free Kids. Ironically, it has also been endorsed by some representatives of the tobacco industry, for example Philip Morris, the largest tobacco company in the United States.

Not everyone supports the legislation, however. In April, 2008, a *Wall Street Journal* editorial claimed that "politicians have dropped public health for public revenue," suggesting that if tobacco is really a serious health threat, stronger measures are needed. State and federal governments, according to the editorial, have come to depend on the sale of tobacco products for tax revenues, and thus are not motivated to address tobacco-related health threats with measures that are proportional to the dangers. The *Wall Street Journal* editorial also claimed that the Family Smoking Prevention and Tobacco Control Act supports monopolistic practices by big tobacco, by shielding existing products from FDA review while allowing close FDA oversight of new product development, including development of so-called "harm-reduction" products. This puts smaller tobacco companies, and newer companies, at a competitive disadvantage, and stifles innovation.

The Family Smoking Prevention and Tobacco Control Act, which would grant the FDA authority to regulate tobacco products, is currently under consideration in the U.S. House of Representatives and in the Senate.

"For decades the federal government has stayed on the sidelines and done next to nothing to deal with this enormous health problem."

The Food and Drug Administration Should Have the Authority to Regulate Tobacco Products

Edward M. Kennedy

In the following viewpoint, U.S. Senator of Massachusetts Edward M. Kennedy argues in support of S. 625, a Senate bill that would provide the U.S. Food and Drug Administration (FDA) with authority to regulate the tobacco industry. Kennedy states that the tobacco industry has proven itself untrustworthy by misleading consumers, making false claims, concealing the dangers of smoking, and targeting its marketing efforts at children and youth. Because the dangers of smoking are so clearly known, he says, the federal government must give the FDA the tools it needs to fight tobacco use.

Edward M. Kennedy, "Remarks of Senator Edward M. Kennedy in Support of FDA Regulation of Tobacco Products," July 25, 2007. http://help.senate.gov. Reproduced by permission.

As you read, consider the following questions:

1. What are some of the organizations that join Senator Kennedy in his support of the Senate bill (S. 625) that would give the Food and Drug Administration the authority to regulate the manufacture and sale of tobacco products?

2. How does Senator Kennedy say the government will pay for the regulatory costs of the proposed tobacco legislation?

3. In nearly every state, it is illegal to sell cigarettes to anyone under the age of eighteen. Senator Kennedy points out that these laws are rarely enforced. How does he propose to reduce the number of cigarette sales to minors?

The Senate is taking the first step toward passage of legislation that should have been enacted years ago—authority for the FDA [U.S. Food and Drug Administration] to regulate tobacco products, the most lethal of all consumer products. Used as intended by the companies that manufacture and market them, cigarettes will kill one out of every three smokers. Yet, the federal agency most responsible for protecting the public health is currently powerless to deal with the enormous risks of tobacco use. Public health experts overwhelmingly believe that passage of [Senate bill] S. 625 is the most important action Congress can take to protect children from this deadly addiction. If Congress fails to act and smoking continues at its current rate, more than six million of today's children will ultimately die from tobacco-induced disease.

Congress Must Act

Smoking is the number one preventable cause of death in America. Nationally, cigarettes kill well over four hundred thousand people each year. That is more lives lost than from automobile accidents, alcohol abuse, illegal drugs, AIDS, murder, and suicide combined. Congress cannot continue to ignore a public health problem of this magnitude.

And Congress will not ignore it. This legislation has broad bipartisan support. Fifty-two Senators have co-sponsored it, including 12 Republicans. They recognize that giving FDA authority over tobacco products is essential to effectively addressing the tobacco health crisis.

The American Cancer Society, the American Heart Association, the American Lung Association, the American Medical Association, the Campaign for Tobacco-Free Kids and dozens of other major public health organizations speak with one voice on this issue. They are all supporting S. 625 because they know it will give the FDA the tools it needs to reduce youth smoking and help addicted smokers quit.

A landmark report by the Institute of Medicine, released [in 2007], strongly urged Congress to "confer upon the FDA broad regulatory authority over the manufacture, distribution, marketing and use of tobacco products."

Opponents of this legislation argue that FDA should not be regulating such a dangerous product. I could not disagree more. It is precisely because tobacco products are so deadly that we must empower America's premier public health protector—the FDA—to combat tobacco use. For decades the federal government has stayed on the sidelines and done next to nothing to deal with this enormous health problem. The tobacco industry has been allowed to mislead consumers, to make false health claims, to conceal the lethal contents of their products, to make their products even more addictive, and worst of all—to seduce generations of children into a lifetime of addiction and early death. The alternative to FDA regulation is more of the same. Allowing this abusive conduct by the tobacco industry to go unchecked would be terribly wrong.

Under this legislation, FDA will for the first time have the needed power and resources to take on this challenge. The cost will be funded entirely by a new user fee paid by the to-bacco companies in proportion to their market share. Not a single dollar will be diverted from FDA's existing responsibilities.

Giving FDA authority over tobacco products will not make the tragic toll of tobacco use disappear overnight. More than forty million people are hooked on this highly addictive product and many of them have been unable to quit despite repeated attempts. However, FDA action can play a major role in breaking the gruesome cycle that seduces millions of teenagers into a lifetime of addiction and premature death.

What Can FDA Regulation Accomplish?

- It can reduce youth smoking by preventing tobacco advertising which targets children.

- It can help prevent the sale of tobacco products to minors.

- It can stop the tobacco industry from continuing to mislead the public about the dangers of smoking.

- It can help smokers overcome their addiction.

- It can make tobacco products less toxic and less addictive for those who continue to use them.

- And it can prohibit unsubstantiated health claims about supposedly "reduced risk" products, and encourage the development of genuinely less harmful alternative products.

Regulating the conduct of the tobacco companies is as necessary today as it has been in years past. The facts presented in the federal government's landmark lawsuit [settled in 1998] against the tobacco industry conclusively demonstrate that the misconduct is substantial and ongoing. The decision of the Court states: "The evidence in this case clearly establishes that Defendants have not ceased engaging in unlawful activity. . . .Defendants continue to engage in conduct that is materially indistinguishable from their previous actions, activity that continues to this day." Only strong FDA regulation can force the necessary change in their corporate behavior.

We must deal firmly with tobacco company marketing practices that target children and mislead the public. The Food and Drug Administration needs broad authority to regulate the sale, distribution, and advertising of cigarettes and smokeless tobacco.

The tobacco industry currently spends over thirteen billion dollars each year to promote its products. Much of that money is spent in ways designed to tempt children to start smoking, before they are mature enough to appreciate the enormity of the health risk. Four thousand children have their first cigarette every day, and one thousand of them become daily smokers. The industry knows that nearly 90% of smokers begin as children and are addicted by the time they reach adulthood.

Why Serious Measures Are Needed

Documents obtained from tobacco companies prove, in the companies' own words, the magnitude of the industry's efforts to trap children into dependency on their deadly product. Studies by the Institute of Medicine and the Centers for Disease Control show the substantial role of industry advertising in decisions by young people to use tobacco products.

If we are serious about reducing youth smoking, FDA must have the power to prevent industry advertising designed to appeal to children wherever it will be seen by children. This legislation will give FDA the authority to stop tobacco advertising that glamorizes smoking to kids. It grants FDA full authority to regulate tobacco advertising "consistent with and to the full extent permitted by the First Amendment" [the U.S. Constitution amendment that guarantees freedom of speech].

Why Regulation Is Needed

"This bill is long overdue," said Rep. Henry A. Waxman (D. Calif.), chairman of the House Government Reform Committee and the lead sponsor in the House [of Representatives of a bill to regulate the tobacco industry]. "Despite the fact that cigarettes kill over 400,000 Americans each year, and despite the fact this is the most toxic substance that is sold legally and when used as intended has the potential to kill, there is virtually no regulation of tobacco by the federal government."

Christopher Lee,
"New Push Grows for FDA Regulation of Tobacco,"
The Washington Post, *February 17, 2007.*

FDA authority must also extend to the sale of tobacco products. Nearly every state makes it illegal to sell cigarettes to children under 18, but surveys show that those laws are rarely enforced and frequently violated. FDA must have the power to limit the sale of cigarettes to face-to-face transactions in which the age of the purchaser can be verified by identification. This means an end to self-service displays and vending machine sales. There must also be serious enforcement efforts with real penalties for those caught selling tobacco products to children. This is the only way to ensure that children under 18 are not able to buy cigarettes.

The FDA conducted the longest rulemaking proceeding in its history, studying which regulations would most effectively reduce the number of children who smoke. Seven hundred thousand public comments were received in the course of that rulemaking. [Senator Kennedy is referring to the 1996 FDA Rule, struck down by the Supreme Court—see Chapter Preface.] At the conclusion of its proceeding, the Agency promulgated rules on the manner in which cigarettes are advertised and sold. Due to litigation, most of those regulations were never implemented. If we are serious about curbing youth smoking as much as possible, as soon as possible, it makes no sense to require FDA to reinvent the wheel by conducting a new multi-year rulemaking process on the same issues. This legislation will give the youth access and advertising restrictions already developed by FDA the force of law, as if they had been issued under the new statute. Once they are in place, FDA will have the authority to modify these rules as changing circumstances warrant.

Warnings Should Be Stronger

The legislation also provides for stronger warnings on all cigarette and smokeless tobacco packages, and in all print advertisements. These warnings will be more explicit in their description of the medical problems which can result from tobacco use. The FDA is given the authority to change the text of these warning labels periodically, to keep their impact strong.

The nicotine in cigarettes is highly addictive. Medical experts say that it is as addictive as heroin or cocaine. Yet for decades, tobacco companies vehemently denied the addictiveness of their products. No one can forget the parade of tobacco executives who testified under oath before Congress that smoking cigarettes is not addictive [in the lawsuits collectively settled in the 1998 Tobacco Master Settlement Agreement]. Overwhelming evidence in industry documents obtained through the discovery process proves that the companies not only knew of this addictiveness for decades, but actually relied on it as the basis for their marketing strategy. As we now know, cigarette manufacturers chemically manipulated the nicotine in their products to make it even more addictive.

A newly released analysis by the Harvard School of Public Health demonstrates that cigarette manufacturers are still manipulating nicotine levels. Between 1998 and 2005, they significantly increased the nicotine yield from major brand name cigarettes. The average increase in nicotine yield over the period was 11%.

The tobacco industry has a long, dishonorable history of providing misleading information about the health consequences of smoking. These companies have repeatedly sought to characterize their products as far less hazardous than they are. They made minor innovations in product design seem far more significant for the health of the user than they actually were. It is essential that FDA have clear and unambiguous authority to prevent such misrepresentations in the future. The largest disinformation campaign in the history of the corporate world must end.

Addressing Addiction

Given the addictiveness of tobacco products, it is essential that the FDA regulate them for the protection of the public. Over forty million Americans are currently addicted to cigarettes. No responsible public health official believes that cigarettes should be banned. A ban would leave forty million people without a way to satisfy their drug dependency. FDA should be able to take the necessary steps to help addicted smokers overcome their addiction, and to make the product less toxic for smokers who are unable or unwilling to stop. To do so, FDA must have the authority to reduce or remove hazardous ingredients from cigarettes, to the extent that it becomes scientifically feasible. The inherent risk in smoking should not be unnecessarily compounded.

Recent statements by several tobacco companies make clear that they plan to develop what they characterize as "reduced risk" cigarettes. Some are already on the market making unsubstantiated claims. This legislation will require manufacturers to submit such "reduced risk" products to the FDA for analysis before they can be marketed. No health-related claims will be permitted until they have been verified to the FDA's satisfaction. These safeguards are essential to prevent deceptive industry marketing campaigns, which could lull the public into a false sense of health safety.

This legislation will vest FDA not only with the responsibility for regulating tobacco products, but with full authority to do the job effectively. It is long overdue.

Enacting this bill this year is the right thing to do for America's children. They are depending on us. By passing this legislation, we can help them live longer, healthier lives.

> *"[This] bill would attempt to apply current requirements for medical products such as drugs and medical devices to tobacco products. . . .Tobacco products, however, are intrinsically injurious to health."*

The Food and Drug Administration Should Not Be Responsible for Regulating Tobacco

Andrew C. von Eschenbach

In his testimony before a subcommittee of the U.S. House of Representatives, Andrew C. von Eschenbach, the U.S. Food and Drug Administration (FDA) commissioner of food and drugs, maintains that House of Representatives bill (H.R. 1108), the "Family Smoking Prevention and Tobacco Control Act," undermines the historical mission and role of the Food and Drug Administration by requiring it to approve a product that is widely known to be dangerous to health. Eschenbach argues that if the

Andrew C. von Eschenbach, "Statement of Andrew C. von Eschenbach, M.D., Commissioner of Food and Drugs, before Subcommittee on Health Committee on Energy and Commerce United States House of Representatives, on H.R. 1108, Family Smoking Prevention and Tobacco Control Act," October 3, 2007. www.fda.gov. Reproduced by permission.

FDA is required to regulate tobacco products, it will be setting safety standards for a product that has no medical benefits and has already been proven to be injurious to humans.

As you read, consider the following questions:

1. What are the two non-nicotine drug products aimed at helping smokers quit that were FDA approved at the time of this testimony?
2. How many states have laws that ban the sale of tobacco to minors?
3. According to a 2004 Surgeon General's report cited in the viewpoint, how many years of potential life are lost for male and female smokers?

Mr. Chairman and Members of the Subcommittee, I am Andrew C. von Eschenbach, M.D., Commissioner of Food and Drugs at the United States Food and Drug Administration (FDA)....

For the last three decades, I have been engaged in the war on cancer both professionally and personally. Throughout my professional career, I have been privileged to serve in a variety of roles with a similar purpose and commitment—to help assure the health and welfare of patients and the public. As many of you may know, I spent many years at the University of Texas M.D. Anderson Cancer Center as an oncologist, researcher, and educator. In my time as a practicing oncologist, I treated numerous patients suffering the ill effects of tobacco. I came to know first hand the life-threatening conditions caused by tobacco products and the tremendous suffering that is taking a toll on patients, their families and friends, and society as a whole. I then served for four and a half years as Director of the National Cancer Institute (NCI) before coming to FDA as Commissioner. Today, I sit before you as a physician, scientist, clinician, and regulator. As a three time cancer survivor, I am involved not just professionally but am personally committed to the fight against cancer and the resulting suffering and death. I am grateful for this Subcommittee's work in minimizing the effects of tobacco use in this country.

The Health Effects of Tobacco Use Are Real

Although tobacco use has declined in this country, its effects are so detrimental that it remains one of the most important—if not the most important—public health issues we face. The 2004 Surgeon General's Report entitled, "The Health Consequences of Smoking," noted that during the period 1995–1999, smoking caused approximately 440,000 premature deaths in the U.S. annually, leading to 13.2 years of potential life lost for male smokers, and 14.5 years lost for female smokers. The list of diseases and conditions caused by smoking has been expanded to include abdominal aortic aneurysm, acute myeloid leukemia, cervical cancer, kidney cancer, pancreatic cancer, stomach cancer, pneumonia, periodontitis, and cataract. Those are in addition to diseases previously known to be caused by smoking, including bladder, esophageal, laryngeal, lung, oral, and throat cancers, chronic lung diseases, coronary heart and cardiovascular diseases, as well as reproductive effects and sudden infant death syndrome. Tobacco users face nicotine addiction, increased risk of cancer from consumption of carcinogens, increased risk of heart disease from exposure to chemicals, and lung disease resulting from inhaled irritants.

We concur with the Surgeon General's conclusion that measures to prevent smoking need to be a multiplex, integrated strategy and initiatives need to be strong and enforced, especially among adolescents and young adults. FDA must continue to work with the drug and device industries to ensure that smokers have a variety of options to help them treat the problem of nicotine addiction.

Much Is Already Being Done

FDA is privileged to be among the other federal and state agencies that are participating in some way to reduce tobacco use. It is clear, however, that the problem remains. We must continue to be innovative in our approaches and concentrate on achieving results.

Many agencies within the [U.S.] Department of Health and Human Services [which oversees the FDA] are working to address this major public health problem. FDA has worked to help develop and approve nicotine replacement products that help smokers quit, such as nicotine gum and patches, many of which are readily available over the counter to smokers who wish to quit. FDA has approved other drug products that do not contain nicotine that help smokers quit using other modes of action, including bupropion [Wellbutrin] and most recently (spring 2006) varenicline [Chantix]. There are a variety of other non-nicotine containing smoking cessation products in the pipeline in various stages of development.

In addition, the Centers for Disease Control and Prevention (CDC), NCI, the Agency for Healthcare Research and Quality (AHRQ), the Substance Abuse and Mental Health Services Administration (SAMHSA), and the National Institute on Drug Abuse (NIDA) are all actively involved in the fight to reduce tobacco use. These agencies conduct comprehensive tobacco control and prevention programs, which serve to educate the American public on the dangers of tobacco, especially American youth. They conduct surveillance and research and collaborate with public health organizations in the prevention of tobacco use and smoking cessation programs. Finally, the Office of the Surgeon General has been especially active in the campaign against tobacco use by following up the 2004 Report with subsequent studies on the health effects of exposure to second-hand smoke and other efforts.

The states are also engaged in a variety of methods to limit smoking. All fifty states have adopted legislation prohibiting sales of tobacco to individuals under 18. Many states also limit smoking in some public locations. Most state health

Copyright © 2004 by Mike Keefe and CagleCartoons.com.

departments run educational programs aimed at prevention and limiting the number of smokers.

Despite the numerous federal and state initiatives, tobacco still claims hundreds of thousands of lives every year. This is unacceptable. We have the opportunity here to explore novel solutions to the lingering problem of tobacco.

The Proposed Legislation Is Flawed in Three Ways

FDA shares the goal of H.R. 1108, the "Family Smoking Prevention and Tobacco Control Act,"—to reduce tobacco use in this country. We agree with the need to address this significant public health problem. But we have concerns with the bill's proposed means to achieve those objectives. The [FDA] has three primary categories of concern with the proposed role for FDA.

First, we have concerns that the bill could undermine the public health role of FDA. Second, we have concerns about aspects of the bill that may be extremely difficult for FDA to implement. And third, we have significant concerns about the resources that would be provided under the bill and the expectations it might create. Let me elaborate on each of those areas.

First, FDA is a public health agency, structured to facilitate and regulate the development of products that promote and protect the public health. The [FDA] enjoys widespread public support for its role in defining and assuring effectiveness and safety of products they consume. Our responsibility includes approving products based on scientific evidence that benefits of the product outweigh the risks. We have extensive experience in such evaluations and we have developed finely tuned methodologies.

H.R. 1108 would ask us to apply this framework to tobacco products that, when used as intended, produce disease rather than promote health. FDA cannot "approve" a tobacco product in this context, because there is no scientific context to determine benefit to outweigh the numerous risks. It will be very challenging to transform existing science into a logical regulatory structure. There is little science available to the FDA on which to base decisions on tobacco product standards (such as reducing or eliminating harmful constituents, reducing the amount of nicotine in products, or requiring changes to tobacco product components) or pre-market approval.

Associating the [FDA] with the approval of these inherently dangerous products would undermine the [FDA's] mission. Indeed, associating any agency whose mission is to promote public health with the approval of inherently dangerous products would undermine its mission and likely have perverse incentive effects. This proposed legislation would direct FDA to regulate tobacco products in a variety of ways, most significantly by the establishment of tobacco product standards, pre-market approval of new tobacco products, and standards for the sale of modified risk tobacco products. Approval of tobacco products that are dangerous to health even if used as directed runs directly counter to FDA's historical mission to protect and promote the public health by reviewing and approving products that prevent and treat disease, not products whose only impact on health is to cause disease.

In addition, the provisions authorizing pre-market approval of new and reduced risk tobacco products are of special concern. Most fundamentally, we are concerned that FDA "approval" of tobacco products may become confused with the [FDA's] regulation of therapeutic products such as drugs and devices. For example, the bill provides potential loopholes for "grandfathered" [exempted because of previously legal status] and "substantially equivalent" products, which will be permitted to stay on the market. We are concerned that the public will believe that products "approved" by the [FDA] are safe and that this will actually encourage individuals to smoke more rather than less.

As another example, the bill would attempt to apply current requirements for medical products such as drugs and medical devices to tobacco products. These include adverse event reporting, adulteration and misbranding, and *record keeping*. These concepts are not applicable to inherently dangerous tobacco products. One example of the awkwardness of applying medical product standards to tobacco products is contained in the bill's definition of an adulterated tobacco product. Section 902 of the bill provides that a "tobacco product shall be deemed to be adulterated if—(1) it consists in whole or in part of any filthy, putrid, or decomposed substance, or is otherwise contaminated by any added poisonous or added deleterious substance that may render the product injurious to health."

Tobacco products, however, are intrinsically injurious to health, i.e. adulterated according to this definition. This concept, therefore, does not fit when applied to the regulation of tobacco products. There are other examples in the bill where similar problems would arise.

The bill also appears to call for FDA to perform functions that are outside of the [FDA's] expertise, including, for example to investigate and prevent cigarette smuggling.

The final issue of concern that I would like to discuss today is that of resources and expectations under this bill. As I am sure you are all aware, FDA is operating in a dynamic time. We are striving to meet new challenges. Just last week [September 2007], the President [George W. Bush] signed the Food and Drug Administration Amendments Act of 2007 that will allow us to continue to evolve and undertake our mission of protecting the public health. Were H.R. 1108 enacted, FDA would need to create an entirely new "tobacco center" to implement the detailed program created by the bill.

By far, the most important and daunting challenge would be to develop the expertise necessary to carry out the functions called for by this bill. FDA does not have expertise regarding customarily marketed tobacco products and, therefore, would have to establish an entirely new program and hire new experts. Creating the appropriate organizational structure and hiring experts in the field of tobacco control and related sciences and other experts needed to staff the program at every level is considerably more challenging than simply filling identified vacancies in an existing program.

The provisions in this bill would require substantial resources and FDA may not be in a position to meet all of the activities within the proposed user fee levels. The $85 million in fiscal year (FY) 2008, $175 million in FY 2009, $300 million in FY 2010 and subsequent years of user fees adjusted by an inflation factor, is not sufficient to implement the complex program created by the bill. In addition, the bill does not authorize appropriations for start-up costs that would be associated with establishing a new product center. As a consequence of this, FDA may have to divert funds from its other programs, such as addressing the safety of drugs and food, to begin implementing this program.

Finally, FDA also would need a considerable amount of time to implement the program created by the bill. The legislation authorizes or requires the [FDA] to publish numerous regulations and other documents.

The bill also requires the [FDA], in a short timeframe, to issue a regulation originally published in 1996 that relies on data and information that are a decade old and would need to be updated to reflect the latest science. Many of the timeframes provided, ranging from 30 days to 2 years after the bill is enacted, are unworkable especially considering the expectation that we produce these documents while we are creating an entirely new program from the ground up. These timeframes unduly and unfairly raise the public's expectations about what the [FDA] could accomplish in a given period of time. In the best of circumstances when scientific results point to a clear regulatory approach, rulemaking typically involves at least a three-year process. In situations where the science is less fully developed or the issues are complex or controversial, and both are the case here, regulation development requires much more time.

I share with you the desire to reduce tobacco use in America. FDA believes it can continue to contribute to the decline in tobacco use in keeping with its primary mission by facilitating access to smoking cessation programs and therapies that have evidence of effectiveness, and by supporting sponsors who choose to pursue the development of these products. However, FDA is open to considering other roles for [itself] if appropriate. Let me assure you that FDA is committed to joining you and other government and private organizations in efforts to minimize the devastating effects caused by tobacco use in a manner consistent with the [FDA's] mission.

| "It would be all too easy to convince ju-
rors that granting the FDA jurisdiction
over the manufacture, sale, safety, and
marketing of tobacco products is sufficient to prevent future legal violations."

FDA Regulation Would
Protect Tobacco Companies
from the Threat of Litigation

Michael Siegel

*In the following viewpoint, Michael Siegel argues against legisla-
tion that would give the U.S. Food and Drug Administration
(FDA) the authority to regulate tobacco. FDA regulation, according to Siegel, would provide legitimacy to the manufacture
of unhealthy products. He argues that tobacco companies would
be able to shield themselves from litigation by claiming their
products were manufactured according to standards agreed upon
by the FDA. It would then be difficult or impossible for people
who had been injured by tobacco products to sue manufacturers
and collect punitive damage awards. Michael Siegel is a physician and on the faculty of the Boston School of Public Health.*

Michael Siegel, "FDA Tobacco Legislation Would Solidify Philip Morris' Financial Position by Shielding it from Liability; Why Would Health Groups Want to Do That?" *The
Rest of the Story: Tobacco News Analysis and Commentary*, December 14, 2007. http://
tobaccoanalysis.blogspot.com. Reproduced by permission.

As you read, consider the following questions:

1. According to a report cited in the viewpoint, what is the chief obstacle to the financial stability of the U.S. tobacco company Philip Morris?

2. What are PREPs, and why does Siegel believe they are important for understanding why Philip Morris favors FDA regulation?

3. How, specifically, does the author think the tobacco companies have been helped by the Campaign for Tobacco-Free Kids?

With enemies like the Campaign for Tobacco-Free Kids, American Cancer Society, and American Medical Association, Philip Morris—the nation's largest cigarette manufacturer—doesn't need friends. Its enemies are about to do it the biggest favor imaginable: to solidify its financial well-being by taking care of, once and for all, the significant liability threat that is hanging over the company.

According to a report issued by Zacks financial analysts, the chief obstacle to Philip Morris' financial stability is the continuing litigation threat—especially, the threat of large punitive damage awards. "Zacks senior consumer industry analyst Steven Ralston, CFA, is keeping the shares of cigarette manufacturer Altria Group, Inc. a Sell [a recommendation to sell a stock], especially as its price has crept up in recent weeks. Here are some of the reasons why: Altria Group is the leading domestic tobacco company. The company generates significant cash flow and has a high dividend yield. However, the company is engaged in numerous tobacco liability suits. Several large punitive damage awards have been upheld by appellate courts, especially the $50-million judgment paid out in the Boeken case after the U.S. Supreme Court refused to hear the case. . . .The stock has maintained a low P/E [price-toearnings ratio] due to tobacco-related litigation issues, and has been pressured down to a single digit P/E during times of court case losses."

The Rest of the Story

The FDA tobacco legislation being promoted by the Campaign for Tobacco-Free Kids, American Cancer Society, American Heart Association, American Lung Association, American Medical Association, and many other health and anti-smoking groups would end, once and for all, the significant litigation threat that hangs over Philip Morris and its financial well-being.

While the legislation itself does not directly affect litigation, its effect would be to definitively end the litigation threat by virtually destroying the possibility of large punitive damage awards in pending and future legal cases against the company. Philip Morris could successfully (and correctly) argue that there is no need for punitive damages because the FDA now has full jurisdiction over the company's marketing practices, the sale of cigarettes, and even the ingredients, components, and design of the cigarette. Thus, there is no need to award huge punitive damages to deter future fraudulent activity.

I have testified before many of the juries in these cases, and I can tell you that this argument will be very compelling. Philip Morris tried to use this type of argument with the Engle jury [1999 Florida class action suit against tobacco companies], but it didn't work because expert witnesses like me testified that the Master Settlement Agreement [the large settlement tobacco companies made in 1998 with 46 states] didn't actually regulate the companies or effectively deter future fraudulent actions. In contrast, it would be all too easy to convince jurors that granting the FDA jurisdiction over the manufacture, sale, safety, and marketing of tobacco products is sufficient to prevent future legal violations.

Tobacco Facts

Tobacco use is the single most preventable cause of death and disease in the United States. People begin using tobacco in early adolescence; almost all first use occurs before age 18. An estimated 45 million American adults currently smoke cigarettes. Annually, cigarette smoking causes approximately 438,000 deaths. For every person who dies from tobacco use, another 20 suffer with at least one serious tobacco-related illness. Half of all long-term smokers die prematurely from smoking-related causes. In 2004, this addiction costs the nation more than $96 billion per year in direct medical expenses as well as more than $97 billion annually in lost productivity. Furthermore, exposure to secondhand smoke causes premature death and disease in nonsmokers. In 2005, the Society of Actuaries estimated that the effects of exposure to secondhand smoke cost the United States $10 billion per year.

Centers for Disease Control and Prevention,
"Best Practices for Comprehensive Tobacco Control Programs."
www.cdc.gov.

The companies will be able to successfully use the argument that they are already regulated to stave off injunctive relief and substantial punitive damages in litigation by appealing to jurors' perceptions that the problem is "taken care of." The highly exaggerated claims of the positive public health impacts of this legislation that the health organizations are making are only contributing to this perception.

Moreover, the FDA tobacco legislation would bail out Philip Morris from what I feel is the most threatening potential litigation to the industry in the future and the one about which I believe the industry is most concerned—claims related to potentially reduced exposure products (PREPs). Ultimately, I argue, as bad as people think the status quo might be, the FDA legislation would be far worse.

It is the status quo—specifically, the absence of FDA regulation of tobacco products—that is actually the limiting factor in the inability or reluctance of tobacco companies to proceed wholeheartedly with the development, introduction, and marketing of PREPs.

This is because of the fear that cigarette companies might face litigation based on claims that they made misleading or unproven health claims about these potentially reduced exposure products. Because it would take years of epidemiologic research after the introduction of these products to provide any meaningful evidence that there is a health benefit from these products compared to existing cigarettes, it is virtually impossible for the cigarette companies to make any health claims regarding PREPs without facing the risk of litigation based on a claim that they are making misleading or unproven health claims.

After all, if they can't prove a health claim until they market and study a cigarette for 10–20 years, and they can't market a PREP until they can prove the health claims, then they are in a complete bind.

But the FDA legislation would bail them out. How? By regulating the introduction and marketing of PREPs, including the conditions regarding the cigarette companies' ability to make various types of health claims, the proposed FDA legislation would preempt any claims against the industry related to PREPs, and would therefore effectively provide immunity for them, allowing them to proceed with the widespread introduction of PREPs into the market, both nationally and internationally.

In essence, not only is the Campaign for Tobacco-Free Kids working to open up global markets to the introduction of a new cigarette innovation that kills people, but does so by making them think they are protecting their health[;] it is also working to take away the legal rights of American citizens to hold corporations accountable for damages suffered as a result of using their products.

With "enemies" like the Campaign for Tobacco-Free Kids, the major cigarette companies do not really need friends—the Campaign is doing their bidding for them in the halls of Congress.

And the result of that bidding, if successful, would be the global expansion of the cigarette market, the third major cigarette product innovation by the industry in the past half a century, the provision of immunity to cigarette companies to introduce and market a broad new class of deadly products with no fear of liability, the widespread introduction and sanctioning by the government of unproven and undocumented health claims that are sure to mislead millions of smokers, and ultimately, needless deaths due to the undermining of public health efforts to encourage smoking cessation, emphasize the deadly effects of cigarette smoking, and ensure that the public is not led to believe that there is any safe cigarette.

The real question is why would these health groups want to do such a favor for Philip Morris?

Perhaps it's because they feel, subconsciously, that they will be getting something in return.

> *"The legislation, which on its surface appeared to advance a health policy goal, aided tobacco interests in avoiding seriously damaging regulation."*

FDA Regulation of Tobacco Would Unfairly Benefit the Largest Tobacco Companies

Joseph A. Rotondi

In the following viewpoint, Joseph A. Rotondi argues that U.S. Food and Drug Administration (FDA) regulation of tobacco, which is favored by "Baptists" (people who want to improve the world) as well as by "bootleggers" (people who hope to profit from a less competitive environment), would not be good economic policy. The real winners in the battle to regulate tobacco, he believes, would be the most powerful tobacco companies, who would be able to exploit conditions created by regulation, increasing their profits in an environment that has the appearance of enhanced social responsibility. Joseph A. Rotondi is a legal fellow in the Regulatory Studies Program at the Mercatus Center at George Mason University.

Joseph A. Rotondi, "Bootleggers, Baptists, and Tobacco Regulation," *Regulation*, summer 2007. www.cato.org. Reproduced by permission.

As you read, consider the following questions:

1. What are some of the organizations that, according to Rotondi, favor FDA regulation of tobacco?
2. What did the Surgeon General of the United States do in 1964, and why was it important?
3. Why does the commissioner of the FDA oppose efforts to have the agency regulate tobacco?

Members of both houses of Congress have introduced identical bills to include tobacco under the Food and Drug Administration's regulatory umbrella. FDA [commissioner] Andrew von Eschenbach opposes this legislation. Altria, the largest U.S. cigarette producer with 51 percent of the market, supports it. This seeming paradox grows from and is explained by tobacco roads paved with "bootlegger-Baptist" coalitions.

The Theory

Pioneered by Bruce Yandle. . .in 1983, "bootleggers and Baptists" is an important addendum to public choice theory [an economic theory that studies the behavior of public officials]. It draws its name from stories behind states' enactment of Sunday alcohol sale prohibition laws. To wit: for moral reasons, Baptists advocated bans on Sunday alcohol sales. Bootleggers [who sell whiskey illegally] quietly and willingly went along for the higher prices and enhanced profit that would result from halted competition. The theory's essence, then, is that durable social regulation forms when two very different groups demand regulation: Baptists' public interest cloaks bootleggers' naked greed, the invisible coalition greases government machinery, and voilà.

The history of U.S. tobacco regulation is rife with these alliances. It has taught some public health advocates, as well as some tobacco companies, that "bootleggers" will likely benefit from FDA control.

Early Bootleggers

Before the 1964 surgeon general's report on smoking's perverse health effects, the cigarette industry largely avoided regulation for two main reasons. First, smoking was a popular and accepted habit. During World War I, the U.S. troop commander in France cabled Washington that "tobacco is as indispensable as the daily ration; we must have thousands of tons of it and without delay." During World War II, tobacco farmers stayed home because their crop was deemed essential to the war effort. After the war, cigarette popularity increased even more, with famous athletes and movie stars lighting up.

Second, industry power pervaded government. Members from tobacco-producing states chaired one third of House [of Representatives] committees and nearly a quarter of Senate committees in the early 1960s. In 1957, one House subcommittee introduced a bill that would have both set limits on tar and nicotine levels in cigarettes and granted the Federal Trade Commission [FTC] injunctive powers to prevent deceptive advertising. Directly thereafter, the subcommittee chairman lost his post and his subcommittee was disbanded altogether. The bootleggers had simply flexed their muscle without concern for Baptist cover.

But in February 1960, the FTC announced it had negotiated a "voluntary agreement" with the industry to cut all tar and nicotine claims from cigarette advertising. Public health Baptists, whose ranks had grown with mounting medical evidence that smoking causes cancer, claimed victory. The FTC chairman called the agreement "a landmark example of industry-government cooperation in solving a pressing problem." But bootleggers had won. While FTC intent was to improve the market for safer cigarettes, the ban forced tobacco companies to stop competing on the health claim margin. As a result, they cut costs and increased profit.

Congress and the Tobacco Industry

There is extensive regulation of the tobacco industry and the cigarettes it produces at every level of government. Perhaps no other product is regulated in so many ways, or by so many agencies, as tobacco products. Moreover, while regulation of consumer products is typically left to federal agencies, Congress itself has stepped in to oversee the tobacco industry in many areas, and during the past 30 years Congress has held frequent hearings to consider whether additional regulation may be warranted. From the seed-bed to the sales counter tobacco products are among the most highly regulated products in the nation.

R.J. Reynolds Tobacco Company. www.rjrt.com.

Baptists Rally, Bootleggers Win

In 1964, the surgeon general issued a major report that linked smoking to lung cancer, chronic bronchitis, and coronary disease. It dramatically changed the political debate on tobacco and stoked Baptist fervor. The FTC quickly issued a rule that would require cigarette ads and packages to say "Cigarette Smoking Is Dangerous to Health and May Cause Death from Cancer and Other Diseases."

The bootleggers took control of this Baptist revival. Through congressional maneuvering, the tobacco industry helped pass a bill that gave the FTC specific authority to regulate health claims and nicotine content in advertising but watered down the FTC warning to read "Caution: Cigarette Smoking May Be Hazardous to Your Health." More importantly, it preempted any further FTC, state, or local government-mandated cigarette package warnings and prohibited any such requirement in cigarette advertising until

1969. The legislation, which on its surface appeared to advance a health policy goal, aided tobacco interests in avoiding seriously damaging regulation.

As adverse health data proliferated, the FTC reversed its ban on tar and nicotine level advertising and created a laboratory to produce standard tar and nicotine measures in various brands. After it published the tar and nicotine data, the companies together agreed in 1971 to disclose those levels in their advertising. This public health regulation once again helped, rather than hurt, tobacco. Publishing federally-certified numbers seemed to imply that the federal government was exercising oversight and that the yields were not severely troubling. Moreover, working with the FTC helped tobacco stave off more threatening FDA regulation.

Baptists Persist

Baptists tried another tack. In June 1967, the Federal Communications Commission [FCC] ruled that the "fairness doctrine" applied to cigarette commercials. That is, radio and television stations that aired cigarette advertisements had to provide free, each week, "a significant amount of time for the other viewpoint." In 1968 alone, the major networks aired 1,300 anti-smoking messages. When per-capita cigarette sales dropped somewhat, the FCC in 1969 issued a new proposal that would have completely prohibited cigarette advertising on television and radio. Around the same time, the FTC proposed a rule to require that all cigarette advertising contain perhaps the most direct and stern warning yet: "Cigarette Smoking Is Dangerous to Health and May Cause Death from Cancer, Coronary Heart Disease, Chronic Bronchitis, Pulmonary Emphysema, and Other Diseases."

Congress again intervened. Representatives of tobacco-producing states introduced bills to prevent the stronger warning label and make permanent the temporary ban on state and federal regulation of cigarette advertising. This time, however, the situation had changed—health legislation was becoming good politics. Thus, after extensive negotiations, the bill that emerged banned all cigarette advertising on electronic media and mildly strengthened the package warning. Baptists had ostensibly won.

In keeping with the prevailing pattern, however, bootleggers gained in at least four ways. First, banning TV ads eliminated the fairness doctrine-mandated public service announcements. Second, eliminating TV ads saved the industry the $200 million annually spent on advertising at the time. Third, the TV ban enabled existing producers to maintain market share because the legislation denied competitors an effective means to establish a brand. Finally, cigarette sales actually increased following the legislation.

In essence, each time Baptist public health advocates gained ground during this period, the large tobacco bootleggers slid in to benefit from cost savings, decreased competition, and the like. But the biggest bootlegger triumph was yet to come.

The Master Settlement Agreement

By the mid-1990s, class actions [lawsuits brought by groups of people] and leaked incriminating documents had cracked tobacco's armor and ended 40 years of plaintiff suit losses against "Big Tobacco." In 1996, Liggett Tobacco Company settled a case and became the first cigarette company ever to do so. That same year, an individual plaintiff won a $750,000 jury award. By 1997, the six largest tobacco companies spent $600 million per year on legal bills, and half of the nation's largest law firms worked tobacco defense. At the same time, anti-tobacco Baptist crusader and FDA [commissioner] Dr. David Kessler independently asserted regulatory jurisdiction over tobacco. (The Supreme Court overturned this attempt in 2000.)

Pressure mounted when a large majority of state attorneys general and their hired private law firms sued the tobacco companies to recover past state Medicaid [federal health program for those with low income] payments to treat smoking-related diseases. The final result topped all previous bootlegger-Baptist coalitions. In November 1998, 46 state attorneys general and the four largest tobacco companies signed the Master Settlement Agreement (MSA), which gave state governments more than $200 billion over 25 years, attorneys general (often looking for elevation to governor) white knight reputations for taking down an "evil" industry, and politically-connected plaintiffs' attorneys more than $11 billion. These "televangelists" rallied Baptist health interest groups to their cause in supposed opposition to the bootlegger industry.

But the MSA, through a series of measures designed to penalize non-participating companies, created an industry cartel that allowed signatory companies to raise prices in concert to cover yearly payments to states. Essentially a cigarette tax through litigation, the price increases meant continued industry profits and transfer of wealth from the least represented party in the settlement—consumers—to states and private attorneys. Baptists cried foul. But after the dust settled and the spoils had been distributed, the televangelists had disappeared to more lucrative pulpits. Though the MSA has since come under attack in courts and has shown minor holes even for the bootlegger companies (e.g., a small but significant decrease in market share), the episode largely allowed them to prevent catastrophe.

The Argument Against Regulation

The current bill in Congress has support from Baptists such as the Campaign for Tobacco-Free Kids and the American Heart Association, former FDA [commissioner] Kessler, and 77 percent of American voters. Even the Southern Baptist Convention's president wants the legislation.

In contrast, current FDA [commissioner] von Eschenbach seems to have learned from the mistakes of FCC, FTC, and FDA chairmen past. FDA regulation will likely be dominated by the most politically connected tobacco companies, which will be able to increase or at least maintain market share as regulation does what it usually does when bootleggers and Baptists connect: cut competition. Further, FDA regulation may have the soothing effect that the FTC's published tar and nicotine statistics had in the early 1970s; as von Eschenbach notes, "What I don't want to see happen is that we are in a position where we are determining that a cigarette is safe."

In the current debate, members of Congress must decide whether they want victory for the largest U.S. cigarette producers at consumer and perhaps even Baptist expense. While they choose, they should bear in mind the historical reality that in the tobacco context, as Baptist fervor foments, bootleggers rake in the alms.

> *"Tobacco politics should go through a 12-step program that can bring it back to the sobriety of coherence and reason."*

The FDA Tobacco Bill Is a Misguided Piece of Legislation

Forces International

In the following viewpoint, Forces International argues that the most recent proposal for U.S. Food and Drug Administration (FDA) regulation of tobacco products is badly written, scientifically confused, and filled with contradictions. For example, the bill advocates measures to reduce the amount of nicotine in cigarettes, when a number of authorities have called for increased levels of nicotine in order to reduce the toxicity of cigarettes. Forces International believes that tobacco control is a failure, and it proposes a 12-step program to restore integrity to public discussion of the health effects of tobacco use. Forces International is a nonprofit organization founded on the principles of libertarianism.

Forces International, "The FDA Tobacco Bill: An Opportunity for a 12-step Program to Heal from Institutional Addiction," January 3, 2007. http://forces.org/Archive. Copyright © 2007 Forces, Inc. Reproduced by permission.

As you read, consider the following questions:

1. According to the authors of this viewpoint, what is the position of the Institute of Medicine on how to increase the safety of cigarettes?

2. Only one cigarette manufacturer supports FDA regulation of the tobacco industry, according to the authors. Which cigarette manufacturer supports the bill?

3. Why does FORCES International object to the language of current anti-smoking campaigns?

Reading the latest FDA [U.S. Food and Drug Administration] Tobacco bill [giving the FDA regulatory power over tobacco products] is no fun—not only because it is a heavy legal document, but especially because of the strident contradictions it contains. It seems to be a pastiche of concepts and rhetoric stolen from a great number of pre-existing documents, pasted together to feed the hungry antismoking beasts in the political forest. But some new and previously ignored concepts have also made it in—concepts that could be somewhat revolutionary for tobacco policy. That the document is loaded with confusion and contradictions and thus dangers and opportunity makes its exploration worthwhile.

The drafters of the document have not explored the implications of much of what they put forward. The proposal that *"Cigarette standards will include provisions for the reduction of nicotine"* would favour an illegal market and is contrary to the scientific evidence that nicotine is safe and that high nicotine in smoke will reduce inhalation and thus risk. Such are the conclusions of the Institute Of Medicine (IOM) Report—to which the bill later on (page 100, line 12) defers on all scientific questions. The proposal on reducing nicotine also contradicts the general tone of the proposed legislation, which does not seem to be hostile to nicotine.

What the Tobacco Bill Requires

The bill directs that "*the regulations or guidance issued under paragraph (1) shall be developed in consultation with the Institute of Medicine, and with the input of other appropriate scientific and medical experts, on the design and conduct of such studies and surveillance.*" Let it be clear, once again, that the Institute of Medicine Report endorses the concept of a safer cigarette that reduces inhalation through *increased delivery of nicotine*. That report has been ignored for over five years by antismoking groups that continued to repeat, endlessly, that nicotine is "one of the most addictive substances known".

The incoherence is not over. The bill would direct the Tobacco Product Scientific Advisory Committee to explore "*whether there is a threshold level below which nicotine yields do not produce dependence on the tobacco products involved*". As there is no real, scientific way to establish "dependence" in the first place—let alone a threshold—it is clear that the existence of any threshold will be the product of arbitrary and ever-changing judgement calls dictated more by beliefs and political, social and financial agendas than by science.

Furthermore, it is stated elsewhere that "*Nicotine is an addictive drug*" and that "*only Congress has authority to remove all nicotine from cigarettes.*" The bill thus *acknowledges the central role of nicotine*—a role that is so paramount, in fact, that only a top political body such as the Congress can have power over it. Moreover, the bill admonishes repeatedly against regulation that would favour the illegal trade, which a reduction of nicotine would certainly do. And it endorses the idea that "*No flavor additives will be added, other than menthol*", a splendid provision to favour an illegal market.

If we try to put those concepts all together to make sense out of them, the bill as it stands comes out as saying something along these lines: Nicotine is an addictive drug and, because of this tremendous power of addiction, smokers keep inhaling deadly toxins and over 400,000 of them die each year.

Therefore, we will try to establish a threshold of that addiction and thus try to reduce the nicotine contents of cigarettes. To that end we will defer to the authority of the IOM, which states that nicotine contents of cigarettes *must be maintained or increased* to reduce inhalation of the toxics, thus obtaining a safer product!

The incoherence and confusion of the antitobacco establishment cannot be more glaring.

The Promise of Risk Reduction

Regardless, the new concept that we see in this bill—a real revolution in the antitobacco industry—is the acknowledgment that a less risky product *can be made.* This alone is a refreshing contrast to all the propaganda and abolitionist philosophy that "a cigarette cannot be safe (or safer)". Of course nothing is (absolutely) "safe", and "safety" has become a rhetorical cultural fixation with chimerical overtones. However, many products can indeed be made to be *safer or less risky*— cigarettes included.

One could argue that the legislative proposal points an accusing finger towards those antismoking groups and public health "authorities" that for decades have suppressed both the development of a safer cigarette and the notion of its feasibility, thus causing. . .an immense number of deaths in the world.

Assuming this as reality and considering that a safer cigarette was conceived, developed and researched by the US National Cancer Institute Smoking and Health Program (killed in 1978 to embrace smoking abolitionism), American and international "public health authorities" are responsible for *the deaths of hundreds of millions.* According to antitobacco's own figures, in fact, if safer cigarettes were introduced in 1980, they would have prevented hundreds of millions of "premature" (whatever that really means) deaths world-wide. It would be nice to see international tribunals at work, now, to bring to

Why Regulation Will Fail

The past 500 years of tobacco control efforts demonstrate that nicotine prohibition is a practical impossibility for numerous reasons, state revenue being one of the most ominous. The FDA [Food and Drug Administration] already has regulatory authority over pharmaceutical grade nicotine products, and requires pharmacists to dispense the most addictive of these only with prescriptions. Meanwhile, every corner store can sell far more addictive and dangerous cigarettes to any adult. The FDA could immediately increase competition between cigarettes and clean nicotine products by approving available nicotine products for over-the-counter sales to adults. Similarly permissive regulation of cigarettes and addictive nicotine products will reduce tobacco use and improve smokers' health, but increase nicotine use in the population. Fortunately, restricted youth access and accurate labeling of nicotine's absolute risks will dissuade many nonsmokers from experimenting with it, while accurate depiction of its risks relative to cigarette smoking will encourage many smokers to switch. The FDA could take a series of small steps that might ultimately replace a large proportion of cigarette smoking with equally addictive nicotine products, without risking serious public health setbacks. Vaccine, methadone, and injury prevention policies establish relevant public health precedents.

Walton Sumner II,
"Permissive Nicotine Regulation as
Complement to Traditional Tobacco Control,"
BMC Public Health, *2005.*

account those responsible for this state of affairs—but that is just a fantasy: the perpetrators of the virtual carnage get promoted in rank, power, and money instead.

Because Philip Morris [PM] seems to be the only major manufacturer that supports the bill, legitimate suspicions arise that PM is seeking a position of market monopoly. How may PM "put the bag" on smokers, politics and "public health"? From his point of view, tobacco control analyst Michael Siegel points out many of the potential traps of this bill in his piece "Tobacco Bill Would Cause Countless Deaths". Siegel's observations are well-reasoned, and continued with his article "Harvard Report Continues to Deceive". In the latter article Siegel (who is of course in favour of less risky cigarettes) comes to the only possible logical conclusion on how to achieve them: *a safer cigarette is a product with much more nicotine and far less toxic constituents*, although the political opportunity for a safer cigarette based on this principle does not seem to be caught. However, were Siegel to be correct in his interpretation that the bill intends to actually reduce nicotine content, that would turn into the greatest public health disaster in history.

A 12-Step Program to Recovery

We have already indicated that this bill is a most visible manifestation of the intellectual, moral, and rhetorical enmeshment of a movement that is utterly drunk with nihilism, abolitionism, moral poisoning and prohibition. But there is still hope for recovery. To recover, the tobacco politics should go through a 12-step program that can bring it back to the sobriety of coherence and reason. To that end many political admissions (or even confessions?) must be forthcoming:

1. The official admission of the dramatic failure of the tobacco control goal of a "smoke-free America by the year 2000", swept under the rug along with the information that nicotine is not a dangerous substance. The fact that about 1/3 of the adult population still smokes in the United States does not mean a failure of "public health" but rather a failure of the concept of social engineering propaganda.

2. The admission that smoking is part of the culture and of the way of life of millions, and that it is a simple but important reward that over a billion people in the world share and *don't intend to surrender.*

3. That such reward is so important for smokers (and, in a climate of persecution, so much identified with personal liberty and self-determination) that they endure the frustration, humiliation, harassment, segregation and social "denormalization" programmes perpetrated against them and carried out by dishonest and obtuse "authorities" all over the world.

4. "Pro-smoking" groups should admit that cigarettes constitute an *increased statistical risk* and—on top of the rights issue and of the fight against the passive smoke fraud—they should demand, *as consumers and in unison, the production of a safer cigarette based on more nicotine and lower toxic constituents. The production of a cigarette that keeps the characteristics of a normal cigarette* (burning, flavour, and actual smoke inhalation) and not those of a "nicotine delivery device". The latter is more associated with syringes and heroin than with a time-honoured habit and ritual which, once devoid of risky components, is also capable of delivering psychological and physical benefits to the consumer besides pleasure and joy of living.

5. Smokers should also be prepared to *change and adapt their tastes and preferences*—and abandon the stiff "loyalty" to a particular brand or type which is typical of so many of them.

6. The antitobacco campaigns laden with rhetoric, instigation, false information, exaggeration, hatred, "denormalization", fear and social pressures should stop—along with smoking bans—to reduce/eliminate social and emotional hysteria. The social environment should be

relaxed and normalized to *prepare for the acceptance of a new, safer product.* It is essential that smokers, as a group, *do not feel pressured or driven into a decision,* but adopt the new product(s) truly *by their own volition,* thus ensuring stability of choice and avoiding the temptation to turn to a black market environment to obtain "the good stuff"—for *the good stuff may well become the safer product.*

7. If smoking were as deadly as they say it is (a position that—we emphasize—*we do not share* as there are *only statistical bases with a multiplicity of co-factors*), the marketing of a product based on high nicotine content greatly reducing the inhalation of toxics *makes sense even in the absence of epidemiological studies.* These studies (by their very nature) not only require time, but *would not be able to reliably measure improvements* (unless they could freeze time and any change in society and environment for about 20 years), let alone reliably account for a myriad of confounders.

8. Coherence with the point above demands an *immediate end* of all misinformation and scare propaganda against nicotine and its "addictiveness". The whole "addictiveness" rhetoric should be dropped—along with the anti-smoking "education" against it directed to young and old: *smoking must go back to being a socially accepted way of life worthy of dignity and respect*—but, this time, *with a product that is safer and is getting safer every day* thanks to technological improvements and ever-changing taste and preference of the consumers. Simple logic and common sense dictates that consumers will be willing to adapt their tastes, and demand a safer product without the need of being pushed into a forced choice through behaviour modification programmes.

9. The definition of addiction itself should be revisited and actually re-written—reserving the word only to those substances that are *psycho-toxic*, as they alter personal behaviour in a *socially destructive manner* while producing no scientifically demonstrable benefit for the user. The mere repetition of use or rituals does not constitute addiction, as pleasurable experiences of all kinds *induce the natural desire to repeat the experience*. Even in the presence of compulsion to the use of a substance that not only is harmless, but could even be beneficial (such as nicotine) the negative connotation of the word *addiction* should be avoided—for "addiction" to good things should be at the core of honest public health.

10. Taxation and price policies should be designed to facilitate the use of the safer products. Better yet, prices should be allowed to fluctuate according to a free market. States should be allowed to compete through taxation and in the full respect of freedom of interstate commerce.

11. Advertisement of an ever-safer cigarette should be permitted and encouraged, while allowing endorsement of the safer cigarettes by current public icons. This, along with point (10), is in diametrical opposition to this bill which is not just un-American, but *anti*-American both in spirit and intents.

12. At the same time, "health authorities" should stop the demonization of the tobacco industry along with that of smoking and smokers. All form of antismoking radical postures should be discouraged—and politicians could easily achieve that by *demanding the cutting of public financing to radical antismoking groups*. Instead of demonization, a form of cooperation between industry, health authorities, consumers and media should be encouraged.

The "War on Smoking" Must End

All that, of course, spells out a radical change in approach, politics and philosophy towards the habit—to the point that the very words "antismoking" and "tobacco control" should change their meaning. Better yet, they should be eliminated altogether because of the emotions, obtuseness, resentment and dishonesty they have become synonyms of. They should be replaced with [words like] *risk reduction, social acceptance and cooperation with smokers.* [Smokers] should be heard and respected as *consumers—not addicts—*while *involving them as contributing stakeholders and actors in the process* rather than "passive patients" in need of "therapies", "help" and "preventions" that *they never really asked for.* That would allow this organization and all the other smokers' representatives to stop writing "public health" in quotes and lowercase, and to write it again in capital letters, as respect for the institution would be restored.

The "war on smoking" and smokers must end and be replaced with a cooperation of all to build a product that is safer every day. Wars have always been bad for public health anyway—and that is a fact which is truly scientifically demonstrated.

Periodical Bibliography

The following articles have been selected to supplement the diverse views in this chapter.

Alcoholism & Drug Abuse Weekly	"Congress Moves Closer to Passing Bill on FDA Regulation of Tobacco," October 15, 2007.
Alan Blum	"Smoking Prevention Bill Benefits Tobacco Companies," *Internal Medicine News*, August 15, 2007.
The Buffalo News	"Prohibitionist Bill Ignores Life-Saving Strategy," November 12, 2007.
Convenience Store News	"Public Wants FDA Regulation for Tobacco," July 27, 2007.
Convenience Store News	"NACS Testifies Against FDA Tobacco Regulation," October 4, 2007.
Peter Hardin	"Tobacco Regulation May Promote Smoking, FDA Commissioner Says," *Winston-Salem Journal*, October 4, 2007.
Gardiner Harris	"Path to Tobacco Bill Includes Compromise and Criticism," *New York Times*, July 17, 2007.
Kim Krisberg	"APHA Calls for FDA Tobacco Regulation," *The Nation's Health*, November 2007.
PR Newswire	"If FDA Is 'Broken,' Why Is Congress Focused on Adding Tobacco Regulation to the Agency Rather Than Ensuring the Safety of Food, Drug and Medical Devices in the United States?" March 26, 2008.
Jacob Sullum	"An Epidemic of Meddling: The Totalitarian Implications of Public Health," *Reason*, May 2007.
The Washington Times	"FDA and Tobacco: New Mission a Serious Mistake," December 17, 2007.

OPPOSING
VIEWPOINTS®
SERIES

CHAPTER 4

How Do the Media Impact Individuals' Choices to Smoke or Not Smoke?

Chapter Preface

Cigarette smoking is known to be harmful, and even deadly. On the other hand, the First Amendment to the U.S. Constitution guarantees freedom of speech. It protects the rights of individuals to hear stories, gather information, and make choices about almost every issue that impacts their lives, and it protects commercial speech that is crafted to sell products. Given the importance of good health and free speech as basic societal values, it is inevitable that questions have arisen about the role the media play in encouraging or discouraging tobacco use, and about what role government should play in regulating speech about tobacco.

In 1999, following completion of the Tobacco Master Settlement Agreement (the document dictating the terms of the landmark settlement between tobacco companies and forty-six states), the attorney general of Massachusetts published regulations that would have restricted the outdoor advertising of tobacco products "including advertising in enclosed stadiums and advertising from within a retail establishment that is directed toward or visible from the outside of the establishment, in any location that is within a 1,000-foot radius of any public playground, playground area in a public park, elementary school or secondary school." The regulations also prohibited interior store advertising of cigarettes or smokeless tobacco products within the 1,000-foot zones unless the signs were placed more than five feet from the floor or the store was an adult-only establishment.

In announcing the regulations, the Massachusetts attorney general explained that the state had an interest in eliminating "deception and unfairness in the way cigarettes and smokeless tobacco products are marketed, sold and distributed in Massachusetts" because of "the incidence of cigarette smoking and smokeless tobacco use by children under legal age."

Tobacco manufacturers responded by filing a lawsuit alleging, among other things, that the Massachusetts regulations violated the First Amendment. The U.S. District Court and Court of Appeals sided with the state, concluding that the attorney general had identified a real problem with underage use of tobacco products. Limiting youth exposure to advertising would combat that problem, and since underage smoking was a legitimate concern of the state, restrictions placed on advertising of tobacco products were warranted.

But in 2001, in *Lorillard Tobacco Co. v. Reilly/Altadis U.S.A. Inc. v. Reilly*, the U.S. Supreme Court overruled the lower courts and decided that the Massachusetts restrictions on tobacco advertising were unconstitutional. While the state insisted that its regulations would deter underage smoking, the Court stated that this was an unproven theory, that there was no evidence that the Massachusetts regulations actually accomplished what the state intended, and that therefore restrictions on the speech of the tobacco companies were unjustified.

The question of what role the government should play in regulating the commercial speech of the tobacco industry is closely related to beliefs about how the media impact individuals' choices to smoke or not to smoke. These beliefs are explored in this chapter.

> *"The Canadian government has the power to. . .stop tobacco companies from considering only the direct internal costs of tobacco marketing and oblige them to account for. . .some of the external costs they impose on society."*

Tobacco Advertising Is Harmful to Public Health

Physicians for a Smoke-Free Canada

In the following viewpoint, Physicians for a Smoke-Free Canada argues that tobacco advertising creates false perceptions about smoking, undermines knowledge about the dangers of smoking, and favorably influences public attitudes toward the tobacco industry. The benefits of such advertising outweigh the costs only because tobacco companies are not responsible for the health care costs associated with tobacco use. Public policy to reduce tobacco use should focus on making the tobacco industry bear a heavier economic burden for advertising its products. Tobacco promotions, they suggest, can be banned or taxed, and financial disincentives can be created that increase the costs of promoting to-

Physicians for a Smoke-Free Canada, "Cigarette Marketing in Canada: More Ways to End Tobacco Advertising," June 2007. www.smoke-free.ca/pdf_1/adbrochure-ending advertising.pdf. Reproduced by permission.

bacco use beyond what prudent business decisions would allow. Physicians for a Smoke-Free Canada is a nonprofit organization founded in 1985.

As you read, consider the following questions:

1. How many countries have ratified a treaty that advocates banning tobacco advertising in order to reduce tobacco consumption?

2. What kinds of tobacco advertising are currently allowed under Canadian law?

3. According to the authors, why are penalties needed in addition to a ban to make advertising unprofitable for the tobacco industry?

Tobacco advertising is harmful because it results in more people starting to smoke and fewer people stopping smoking which, in turn, results in more illnesses, deaths, health care costs and bereaved families.

Because tobacco advertising increases smoking, bans on such advertising reduce tobacco use. The World Health Organization recommends banning tobacco advertising. One hundred forty-eight countries—including Canada—have ratified a tobacco treaty which acknowledges that "a comprehensive ban on tobacco advertising, promotion and sponsorship would reduce the consumption of tobacco products."

Tobacco Companies Advertise to Increase Profits

Tobacco companies do not advertise in order to cause more people to become ill or die from smoking cigarettes. This is a consequence of their actions, but not the purpose of them. The primary purpose of tobacco advertising is to increase revenues, and subsequently profits, for the tobacco company shareholders.

By distinguishing between the effect of tobacco advertising (disease and death) and the primary purpose of tobacco advertising (making money) we can strengthen public policy by using both measures which seek to blunt the effect of the cigarette marketing and also measures to amend the motivation that drives the harmful activity of promoting smoking.

Advertising Changes Attitudes Towards Smoking

Advertising helps tobacco companies sell more cigarettes because it:

- *Affects perceptions about smoking*: Promotions create imagery and awareness about brands, but also affect more general perceptions of smoking, its social acceptability, and about the type of people who are addicted to tobacco.

- *Undermines health knowledge by*:

  - providing 'friendly familiarity' about brands and tobacco products *("If cigarettes were really harmful, they wouldn't be advertised in mainstream magazines.")*;

  - providing positive imagery about tobacco brands or about smoking *("If cigarettes were really that harmful, they wouldn't be smoking in movies.")*;

  - creating the impression of normalcy *("If cigarettes were really that harmful, governments wouldn't allow them to be marketed this way.")*

- *Creates allies against public health measures*: Those who benefit economically from tobacco marketing help the companies oppose public health measures aimed at reducing tobacco use. Recent examples include:

  - opposition of retailers to bans on retail displays of cigarettes in Nova Scotia, Quebec, Ontario, Manitoba and Saskatchewan (2000–2006);

165

- opposition of festival organizers to bans on sponsorship advertising (1988–2003);

- opposition of printers and trade unions to new health warning labels (2000).In most cases, tobacco control measures are weakened or postponed as a result of these third-party interventions. These economic relationships are not only forged through direct purchase of advertising space, but also through corporate marketing to the affected sectors. Tobacco companies provide generous sponsorship to trade associations, like convenience retailers, hospitality sectors, etc.

- *Improves public attitudes towards their industry*: The continued presence of corporate names, logos, colours, images and continued portrayal of smoking ameliorates the low public standing of tobacco companies. Through sponsorship of business events, promoting their charitable donations, sponsoring community programmes, hosting dignitaries at sporting events, the companies seek to maintain legitimacy and normalcy within the business sector.

Current Tobacco Product Advertising Today

Canada's 1997 Tobacco Act allows tobacco product advertising:

- in general audience newspapers and magazines (interpreted to include web-sites);

- in direct mail to adults (interpreted to include e-mail);

- in bars and other venues where youth are not allowed;

- through sponsorship, using tobacco company brand names, of certain goods and services that are thought not to appeal to youth, such as taxis, security services or currency exchanges.

Although cigarette manufacturers have refrained from advertising while their court challenge has been heard, other tobacco merchants are using these provisions to market tobacco products. . . .

The Cost-Benefit Decision to Advertise

Cigarette companies advertise only when the benefits of doing so outweigh the costs. Because they can 'externalize' the health care costs that result from the use of their products (that is to say, make smokers, their families and health care providers pay these costs), they need only consider the 'internal' costs. *Internalized* marketing costs include:

- direct financial marketing costs;

- risks to the image of their products or corporation if there is a backlash to their products.

Cigarette advertising is a good business decision for tobacco companies only because the main costs that result from smoking are not paid by the companies. *Externalized* costs that result from tobacco marketing include:

- cost to the cigarette smoker whose cigarettes cost more in order to pay for the advertising;

- cost to the cigarette smoker who pays for more cigarettes as a result of starting smoking or continuing to smoke longer than he or she otherwise would have done;

- costs to the smoker, the smoker's family and the community to pay for health care services for the diseases caused by smoking the additional cigarettes smoked as a result of marketing;

- costs to the smoker, the smoker's family and the community that result from disability, lower productivity and early mortality caused by smoking the additional cigarettes as a result of advertising.

167

Cigarette Advertising in the Nineteenth Century

Taking advantage of the development of color, James B. Dulce revealed his marketing talent with the creation of a whole new way of advertising tobacco and cigarettes. With each pack of cigarettes, a small cardboard insert was added to stiffen the box. Dulce employed a little imagination and turned these simple work-horses into a powerful marketing tool by printing the brand name of the cigarettes along with a picture that was part of a larger series and which was meant to be collected. Series of birds, flags, Civil War generals, and baseball players were employed, frequently with historical or educational information on them. Photographs of "actresses"—women placed in a variety of poses and often rather revealing costumes for the time—also were used on the insert cards and exceeded all expectations in their popularity among the public.

The Tobacco Collections,
Duke University Digital Collections.
http://library.duke.edu.

Public Policy Can Change the Business Decision

Governments can use public policy to change the way tobacco companies behave and also the way they think.

- Public measures can increase the costs of advertising or decrease the benefits so that there is no longer a good business case for advertising. If the costs of advertising outweigh the benefits, advertising will cease. This would prompt a change in *internal calculations.*

- Public measures can shift the requirement to maximize profits into requirements to reduce the number of cigarettes smoked. With such new legal requirements, the industry will not advertise in ways that increase smoking (although they might advertise in ways that decrease smoking). This would prompt a change in *internal motivation*.

Increasing the Costs

The Canadian government has the power to put measures in place which will stop tobacco companies from considering only the direct internal costs of tobacco marketing and oblige them to account for at least some of the external costs they impose on society. Measures which would affect the business decision by increasing the costs of marketing include:

- *Banning tobacco promotions*: A comprehensive ban on marketing with sufficient penalties in place that the industry perceives that the costs of breaching the law or exploring loopholes would exceed any benefits of doing so will make tobacco marketing uneconomic. Such a ban is not currently in place in Canada (the 1997 Tobacco Act allows for advertising in newspapers, magazines, bars, direct mail, web-sites, e-mail, matches and lighters, some non-tobacco goods and services and does little to prevent cross border advertising).

- *Ending financial incentives and creating financial disincentives for marketing*:

  - Removing any corporate income tax relief from promotions (these are currently considered allowable business expenses).

  - Requiring tobacco manufacturers to be licensed, and having a significantly higher license fee for tobacco companies which wish to advertise or promote their products.

- Recouping the externalized costs that result from tobacco marketing. Such approaches have been explored, but not yet put in place in other North American jurisdictions. For example, a 'look-back' provision was included in the (failed) U.S. 'global settlement' with tobacco companies [a proposed settlement that preceded the Master Settlement Agreement of 1998 between the tobacco companies and 46 states]. This would have assessed the companies for the costs of new smokers beyond the threshold percentage of youth smokers estimated without the presence of tobacco marketing. Another example is provided in the [abandoned] British Columbia Tobacco Fee Act of 1999 which imposed a levy on tobacco industry profits in order to pay for the costs to the province of programmes to treat cigarette addiction and to prevent tobacco use.

- Creating financial disincentives for those who supply marketing services to tobacco companies by imposing a surtax on income derived from tobacco promotions, or by using a 'contract compliance' approach to ensure that government business is restricted to companies that do not engage in supplying market research, marketing, advertising, promotion or related services to tobacco companies. Precedents for both these approaches currently exist in Canadian federal government practice.

Decreasing the Benefits

Government measures can be used to ensure that tobacco marketing does not help tobacco companies achieve their marketing goals of:

- influencing public and individual perceptions about smoking or tobacco products;

- impacting on public policy and programs;

- influencing public and individual perceptions about the tobacco industry.

Such government measures include:

Requiring prominent health or other informational messages on direct and indirect advertising: Tobacco advertising which is required to carry large, compensatory health messages will blunt any advertising impact with potential benefit to industry, and consequently make such advertising undesirable to companies. For example, a graphic health warning required on any advertisement or promotion paid for by a tobacco company or another company acting on their behalf that takes up 50% or more of the advertising space will make it unlikely that tobacco companies will find such advertising worthwhile. An example of the impact of such measures was observed in Canada in the early 1990s. During the phase-in period of the [Canadian] Tobacco Products Control Act, companies were required to place 30% health warning messages along the top of any allowed billboards (until the billboards were no longer permitted). The industry responded by terminating their advertising well before they were required to.

Severely limiting the channels of any permitted marketing communications: Permitted advertising can be restricted to specified narrow channels of communication. One example, recommended by the Canadian Cancer Society, is limiting any tobacco promotions to only a binder of informational material maintained behind the counter at cigarette retail outlets.

Plain packaging: Tobacco advertising has traditionally attempted to create an association between a brand image and the branded package. By removing all imagery from the package and reducing the 'brand value' of the package, this connection can be severed or reduced.

Imposing a 'fairness doctrine'-style program of counter-marketing: Tobacco industry promotions and messaging (both brand advertising and corporate promotions) can be countered by making equivalent resources available to public agencies for the purposes of managing counter-advertising programs.

Changing the Internal Motivation

The measures mentioned above are intended to change the way tobacco companies behave. Government also has the power to change the way tobacco companies think. Instead of trying to maximize profits by increasing cigarette sales, the managers of tobacco companies can be legally charged with other goals—such as reducing the number of cigarettes sold.

- *Removing tobacco companies from the requirements of the Corporations Act to act in the "best interests of shareholders"*: Current corporate law requires tobacco companies to act in profit-maximizing ways and this compels them to try to increase sales. A new law could be developed to resolve the conflict between 'best interests of the corporation' and 'best interests of Canadians' with respect to smoking. There are many sectors which have a separate law to govern their business practices for this reason, such as broadcasting, financial institutions and nuclear industries. Government could remove tobacco companies from the list of enterprises governed by the [Canadian] Corporations Act and add the entire tobacco manufacturing sector to the list of industrial sectors governed by industry-specific laws.

- *Imposing production quotas*: Governments can set limits on the number of cigarettes that can be legally sold in a year and alter the financial returns on cigarette sales to encourage reduced production. This can be done by imposing conditions of license on tobacco manufacturers, or by imposing supply-management on tobacco product manufacturing.

- Tobacco companies could be required to achieve progressively lower production and consumption targets every year. If they achieved lower than targeted levels of production and consumption, they could be rewarded with substantial financial bonuses. If, on the other hand, they failed to meet their annual targets, they could face stiff financial penalties. Both the bonuses and penalties would be very substantial, so as to ensure that they would have the desired effect. In such an environment, the only kind of advertising that would make good business sense would be advertising that served to reduce consumption, not increase it.

Measures Available to Government

Changing the way tobacco companies behave:

- Pass a law creating a comprehensive ban on all forms of direct and indirect tobacco advertising, promotion and marketing.

- Guarantee the constitutional validity of such a law. . .by seeking and obtaining the consent of sufficient provincial governments to amend the constitution in order to limit protection of commercial speech to natural persons only (not corporations).

- Failing a comprehensive ban, pass a law banning all but a very few forms of tobacco advertising, i.e. allowing only informational binders behind the counter at point of sales.

- Impose financial disincentives on tobacco marketing through tariffs or license fees, including differential fees for those who wish to advertise.

- Ensure that tobacco companies pick up the otherwise externalized costs of tobacco marketing, through 'lookback' provisions, tariffs or other mechanisms.

- Require prominent health or other informational messages on all forms of tobacco company promotions (including. . .smoking behaviour, such as smoking in movies).

- Require plain packaging of tobacco products.

- Create a 'fairness doctrine'-style program of counter-marketing to ensure that all tobacco product marketing is balanced with public health information.

- Create financial disincentives to recipients of tobacco industry promotional contracts, such as an income sur-tax or ineligibility for government contracts.

Changing the way tobacco companies think:

- Remove tobacco companies from the Corporations Act obligations to act in the 'best interests' of the shareholder.

- Create a supply-management system for tobacco products.

- Introduce requirements for tobacco farmers, manufacturers and importers to achieve annual reductions in tobacco production and consumption.

The Framework Convention on Tobacco Control [FCTC]

In ratifying the FCTC, Canada assumed a number of responsibilities with respect to the control of tobacco. Article 13 of the treaty requires that Canada impose a comprehensive ban on tobacco advertising within the limits of Canada's constitutional principles by February 2010. Although the [Canadian] Supreme Court ruling may clarify the constitutionality of the current Tobacco Act, it is not expected to address whether or not Canada needs to amend its laws in order to meet the requirements of the FCTC.

Whether or not the Supreme Court upholds the Tobacco Act, the government must determine whether a comprehensive advertising ban, as required under the FCTC, is consistent with Canada's constitutional principles and, if so, enact one.

Ways in which such a ban can be established to be consistent with Canada's constitutional principles include:

- a Supreme Court ruling that tobacco advertising is not a form of protected speech (such a position was argued before the court by British Columbia);

- a Supreme Court ruling that tobacco advertising is protected by the charter, but that a comprehensive ban is justified. Although the question of a comprehensive ban is not currently before the court (the Tobacco Act is a partial ban), this question could possibly be determined by the Supreme Court itself, should it volunteer such an opinion in its judgement on the Tobacco Act. Alternatively, it could be determined through a reference question to the court or through subsequent legislation;. . .

- a constitutional amendment to the effect that protected speech is reserved for natural persons, and not for corporations.

"There is remarkably little evidence that people smoke because of messages from tobacco companies."

Tobacco Advertising Does Not Directly Cause People to Smoke

Jacob Sullum

In the following viewpoint, Jacob Sullum disputes the key argument behind restrictions on the advertising of tobacco products: that cigarette ads influence people to smoke. Sullum discusses the backlash over the Joe Camel ad campaign and the subsequent banning of the cartoon image, and points out that the studies that were cited as support for the ban actually proved a very weak association in children's minds between Joe Camel and cigarettes. Sullum says that, in general, analyses of the relationship between advertising and smoking have produced mixed results, and that the link is not significant enough to support a total ban on the ads. Sullum, a senior editor at Reason *magazine, is an author and nationally syndicated columnist.*

Jacob Sullum, "Cowboys, Camels, and Kids: Does Advertising Turn People Into Smokers?" *Reason*, April 1998. Copyright © 1998 by Reason Foundation, 3415 S. Sepulveda Blvd., Suite 400, Los Angeles, CA 90034, www.reason.com. Reproduced by permission.

As you read, consider the following questions:

1. When were the first restrictions on tobacco advertising put into place?

2. What did critics consider to be the main problem with the Joe Camel image?

3. What other factors, besides advertising, contribute to changes in smoking rates?

January 1, 1971, the Marlboro Man rode across the television screen one last time. At midnight a congressional ban on broadcast advertising of cigarettes went into effect, and the smoking cowboy was banished to the frozen land of billboards and print ads. With the deadline looming, bleary-eyed, hungover viewers across the country woke to a final burst of cigarette celebration. "Philip Morris went on a $1.25-million ad binge New Year's Day on the Dick Cavett, Johnny Carson and Merv Griffin shows," *The New York Times* reported. "There was a surfeit of cigarette ads during the screening of the bowl games." And then they were gone. American TV viewers would no longer be confronted by happy smokers frolicking on the beach or by hapless smokers losing the tips of their extra-long cigarettes between cymbals and elevator doors. They would no longer have to choose between good grammar and good taste.

This was widely considered an important victory for consumers. The *Times* wondered whether the ad ban was "a signal that the voice of the consumer, battling back, can now really make itself heard in Washington." A *New Yorker* article tracing the chain of events that led to the ban concluded, "To an increasing degree, citizens of the consumer state seem to be perceiving their ability to turn upon their manipulators, to place widespread abuses of commercial privilege under the prohibition of laws that genuinely do protect the public, and, in effect, to give back to the people a sense of controlling their own lives."

As these comments suggest, supporters of the ban viewed advertising not as a form of communication but as a mysterious force that seduces people into acting against their interests. This was a common view then and now, popularized by social critics such as Vance Packard and John Kenneth Galbraith. In *The Affluent Society* (1958), Galbraith argued that manufacturers produce goods and then apply "ruthless psychological pressures" through advertising to create demand for them. In *The Hidden Persuaders* (1957), Packard described advertising as an increasingly precise method of manipulation that can circumvent the conscious mind, influencing consumers without their awareness. He reinforced his portrait of Madison Avenue guile with the pseudoscientific concept of subliminal messages: seen but not seen, invisibly shaping attitudes and actions. The impact of such ideas can be seen in the controversy over tobacco advertising. The federal court that upheld the ban on broadcast ads for cigarettes quoted approvingly from another ruling that referred to "the subliminal impact of this pervasive propaganda."

Eliminating TV and radio commercials for cigarettes, of course, did not eliminate criticism of tobacco advertising. In 1985 the American Cancer Society, which decades earlier had called for an end to cigarette ads through "voluntary self-regulation," endorsed a government ban on all forms of tobacco advertising and promotion. The American Medical Association, the American Public Health Association, the American Heart Association, and the American Lung Association also began advocating a ban. Beginning in the mid-'80s, members of Congress introduced legislation that would have prohibited tobacco advertising, limited it to "tombstone" messages (black text on a white background), or reduced its tax deductibility. None of these bills got far.

In the '90s, since Congress did not seem inclined to impose further censorship on the tobacco companies, David Kessler, commissioner of the Food and Drug Administration, decided to do it by bureaucratic fiat. Reversing the FDA's longstanding position, he declared that the agency had jurisdiction over tobacco products. In August 1996 the FDA issued regulations aimed at imposing sweeping restrictions on the advertising and promotion of cigarettes and smokeless tobacco. Among other things, the regulations prohibited promotional items such as hats, T-shirts, and lighters; forbade brand-name sponsorship of sporting events; banned outdoor advertising within 1,000 feet of a playground, elementary school, or high school; and imposed a tombstone format on all other outdoor signs, all indoor signs in locations accessible to minors, and all print ads except those in publications with a negligible audience under the age of 18. . . .

These restrictions are based on the premise that fewer ads will mean fewer smokers—in particular, that teenagers will be less inclined to smoke if they are not exposed to so many images of rugged cowboys and pretty women with cigarettes. As a PTA official put it in 1967, "The constant seduction of cigarette advertising. . .gives children the idea that cigarettes are associated with all they hold dear—beauty, popularity, sex, athletic success." For three decades the debate over tobacco advertising has been driven by such concerns. Yet there is remarkably little evidence that people smoke because of messages from tobacco companies. The ready acceptance of this claim reflects a widespread view of advertising as a kind of magic that casts a spell on consumers and leads them astray.

Today's critics of capitalism continue to elaborate on the theme that Vance Packard and John Kenneth Galbraith got so much mileage out of in the '50s and '60s. Alan Thein Durning of the anti-growth Worldwatch Institute describes the "salient characteristics" of advertising this way: "It preys on the weaknesses of its host. It creates an insatiable hunger. And it leads to debilitating over-consumption. In the biological realm, things of that nature are called parasites." When combined with appeals to protect children, this perception of advertising as insidious and overpowering tends to squelch any lingering concerns about free speech.

Busting Joe Camel's Hump

In 1988 R.J. Reynolds gave the anti-smoking movement an emblem for the corrupting influence of tobacco advertising. Introduced with the slogan "smooth character," Joe Camel was a cartoon version of the dromedary (known as Old Joe) that has appeared on packages of Camel cigarettes since 1913. Print ads and billboards depicted Joe Camel shooting pool in a tuxedo, hanging out at a nightclub, playing in a blues band, sitting on a motorcycle in a leather jacket and shades. He was portrayed as cool, hip, and popular—in short, he was like a lot of other models in a lot of other cigarette ads, except he was a cartoon animal instead of a flesh-and-blood human being. Even in that respect he was hardly revolutionary. More than a century before the debut of Joe Camel, historian Jordan Goodman notes, the manufacturer of Bull Durham smoking tobacco ran newspaper ads throughout the country depicting the Durham Bull "in anthropomorphic situations, alternating between scenes in which the bull was jovial and boisterous and those where he was serious and determined."

But Joe Camel, it is safe to say, generated more outrage than any other cartoon character in history. Critics of the ad campaign said the use of a cartoon was clearly designed to appeal to children. *Washington Post* columnist Courtland Milloy said "packaging a cartoon camel as a 'smooth character' is as dangerous as putting rat poison in a candy wrapper." In response to such criticism, R.J. Reynolds noted that Snoopy sold life insurance and the Pink Panther pitched fiberglass insulation, yet no one assumed those ads were aimed at kids.

The controversy intensified in 1991, when *The Journal of the American Medical Association* published three articles purporting to show that Joe Camel was indeed a menace to the

State and Federal Laws Governing Tobacco Product Advertising

- Eight states and the District of Columbia place some restrictions on tobacco advertising and promotion. Furthermore, 21 states and the District of Columbia restrict or virtually prohibit where free samples of tobacco products can be distributed to the general public.

- States are limited in their ability to restrict cigarette advertising and promotion because of a provision in the Federal Cigarette Labeling and Advertising Act, originally passed in 1966, that preempts states and cities from further restricting the time, place and manner of cigarette advertising and promotion. This same legislation was amended in 1971 to ban certain means of advertising concerning cigarettes, such as advertising on radio and television.

- Tobacco companies are allowed to deduct the cost of advertising and promotion from their taxes as a business expense, which saves them in excess of $1 billion a year in taxes.

American Lung Association. www.lungusa.org.

youth of America. The heavily promoted studies generated an enormous amount of press coverage, under headlines such as "Camels for Kids" (*Time*), "I'd Toddle a Mile for a Camel" (*Newsweek*), "Joe Camel Is Also Pied Piper, Research Finds" (*The Wall Street Journal*), and "Study: Camel Cartoon Sends Kids Smoke Signals" (*Boston Herald*). Dozens of editorialists and columnists condemned Joe Camel, and many said he should be banned from advertising.

In March 1992 the Coalition on Smoking or Health, a joint project of the American Cancer Society, the American Heart Association, and the American Lung Association, asked the Federal Trade Commission to prohibit further use of the smooth character. Surgeon General Antonia Novello and the American Medical Association also called for an end to the campaign. In August 1993 the FTC's staff backed the coalition's petition, and a month later 27 state attorneys general added their support. In June 1994, by a 3-to-2 vote, the FTC decided not to proceed against Joe, finding that the record did not show he had increased smoking among minors. (During the first five years of the campaign, in fact, teenage smoking actually declined, starting to rise only in 1993.) In March 1997, after several members of Congress asked the FTC to re-examine the issue, the commission's staff again urged a ban, citing new evidence that R.J. Reynolds had targeted underage smokers. This time the commission, with two new members appointed by the Clinton administration, decided to seek an order instructing RJR not only to keep Joe out of children's sight but to conduct a "public education campaign" aimed at deterring underage smoking.

The two dissenting commissioners were not impressed by the new evidence, which failed to show that Joe Camel had actually encouraged kids to smoke. One wrote, "As was true three years ago, intuition and concern for children's health are not the equivalent of—and should not be substituted for—evidence sufficient to find reason to believe that there is a likely causal connection between the Joe Camel advertising campaign and smoking by children." But the FTC's action turned out to be doubly irrelevant. R.J. Reynolds, along with its competitors, agreed to stop using cartoon characters as part of the proposed nationwide settlement, and last July it announced that it was discontinuing the "smooth character" campaign, replacing it with one that makes more subtle use of camels.

Although the *JAMA* articles were widely cited by Joe's enemies, including the FTC and President Clinton, they proved much less than the uproar would lead one to believe. In the first study, researchers led by Paul M. Fischer, a professor of family medicine at the Medical College of Georgia, asked preschoolers to match brand logos to pictures of products. Overall, about half the kids correctly matched Joe Camel with a cigarette. Among the 6-year-olds, the share was 91 percent, about the same as the percentage who correctly matched the Disney Channel logo to a picture of Mickey Mouse.

But recognizing Joe Camel is not tantamount to smoking any more than recognizing the logos for Ford and Chevrolet (which most of the kids also did) is tantamount to driving. The researchers seemed to assume that familiarity breeds affection, but that is not necessarily the case. A subsequent study, funded by R.J. Reynolds and published in the Fall 1995 *Journal of Marketing*, confirmed that recognition of recognition of Joe Camel rises with age and that most 6-year-olds correctly associate him with cigarettes. Yet 85 percent of the kids in this study had a negative attitude toward cigarettes, and the dislike rose with both age and recognition ability. Among the 6-year-olds, less than 4 percent expressed a positive attitude toward cigarettes. . . .

Does Life Imitate Ads?

Some analyses of historical data have found a small, statistically significant association between increases in advertising and increases in smoking; others have not. In a 1993 overview of the evidence, Michael Schudson, professor of communication and sociology at the University of California at San Diego, wrote, "In terms of a general relationship between cigarette advertising and cigarette smoking, the available econometric evidence is equivocal and the kind of materials available to produce the evidence leave much to be desired." This sort of research is open to challenge on technical grounds, such as the time period chosen and the methods for measuring advertising and consumption. There is also the possibility that advertising goes up in response to a rise in consumption, rather than the reverse. Industry critics often cite the increases in smoking by women that occurred in the 1920s and the late '60s to early '70s as evidence of advertising's power. "Yet in both cases," Schudson noted, "the advertising campaign followed rather than preceded the behavior it supposedly engendered." In other words, the tobacco companies changed their marketing in response to a trend that was already under way.

International comparisons have also produced mixed results. There is no consistent relationship between restrictions on advertising and smoking rates among adults or minors. In some countries where advertising is severely restricted, such as Sweden, smoking rates are relatively low. In others, such as Norway, they are relatively high. Sometimes smoking drops after advertising is banned; sometimes it doesn't. It is hard to say what such findings mean. Countries where smoking is already declining may be more intolerant of the habit and therefore more likely to ban advertising. Alternatively, a rise in smoking might help build support for a ban. Furthermore, advertising bans are typically accompanied by other measures, such as tobacco tax increases and restrictions on smoking in public, that could be expected to reduce cigarette purchases. The one conclusion it seems safe to draw is that many factors other than advertising affect tobacco consumption.

The best way to resolve the issue of advertising's impact on smoking would be a controlled experiment: Take two groups of randomly selected babies; expose one to cigarette advertising but otherwise treat them identically. After 18 years or so, compare smoking rates. Since such a study would be impractical, social scientists have had to make do with less tidy methods, generally involving interviews, questionnaires, or survey data. This kind of research indicates that the most important factors influencing whether a teenager will smoke are the behavior of his peers, his perceptions of the risks and benefits of smoking and the presence of smokers in his home. Exposure to advertising does not independently predict the decision to smoke, and smokers themselves rarely cite advertising as an important influence on their behavior. . . .

Serious critics of tobacco advertising do not subscribe to a simple stimulus-and-response theory in which kids exposed to Joe Camel automatically become smokers. They believe the effects of advertising are subtle and indirect. They argue that the very existence of cigarette ads suggests "it really couldn't be all that bad, or they wouldn't be allowed to advertise," as Elizabeth Whelan of the American Council on Science and Health puts it. They say advertising imagery reinforces the notion, communicated by peers and other role models, that smoking is cool. They say dependence on advertising revenue from tobacco companies discourages magazines from running articles about the health consequences of smoking. They do not claim such effects are sufficient, by themselves, to make people smoke. Rather, they argue that at the margin—say, for an ambivalent teenager whose friends smoke—the influence of advertising may be decisive.

Stated this way, the hypothesis that tobacco advertising increases consumption is impossible to falsify. "Fundamentally," writes Jean J. Boddewyn, a professor of marketing at Baruch College, "one cannot prove that advertising does *not* cause or influence smoking, because one cannot scientifically prove a negative." So despite the lack of evidence that advertising has a substantial impact on smoking rates, tobacco's opponents can argue that we should play it safe and ban the ads—just in case.

The problem with this line of reasoning is that banning tobacco advertising can be considered erring on the side of caution only if we attach little or no value to freedom of speech. If cigarette ads are a bad influence on kids, that is something for parents and other concerned adults to counter with information and exhortation. They might even consider a serious effort to enforce laws against cigarette sales to minors. But since we clearly are not helpless to resist the persuasive powers of Philip Morris et al.—all of us see the ads, but only some of us smoke—it is hard to square an advertising ban with a presumption against censorship. Surely a nation that proudly allows racist fulminations, communist propaganda, flag burning, nude dancing, pornography, and sacrilegious art can safely tolerate Marlboro caps and Joe Camel T-shirts.

> *"[Tobacco companies] intentionally marketed to young people in order to recruit 'replacement smokers' and then denied conducting such marketing efforts."*

The Tobacco Industry's Smoking Prevention Ads Increase the Likelihood That Teens Will Smoke

American Legacy Foundation

In the following viewpoint, the American Legacy Foundation argues that youth smoking prevention ads, such as Philip Morris's "Think. Don't Smoke" campaign, actually increase the likelihood that teens who see the ads will choose to smoke in the future. The tobacco industry has a long history of aiming its marketing efforts at young people, then denying that intention. The recent youth smoking prevention ads need to be seen as another instance of a pattern of predatory and deceptive behavior on the part of tobacco companies, says the American Legacy Foundation, which claims that it and other health-oriented agencies

American Legacy Foundation, "Trick or Treat? Tobacco Industry Prevention Ads Don't Help Curb Youth Smoking and Should Be Taken Off the Air, Says the American Legacy Foundation," PR Newswire, October 31, 2007. Copyright © 2006 PR Newswire Association LLC. Reproduced by permission.

have produced more effective smoking prevention ads. The American Legacy Foundation was created with funds from the Master Settlement Agreement with the tobacco companies and its mission is to stop and to prevent tobacco use.

As you read, consider the following questions:

1. Who is the target audience for the smoking prevention ads produced by the tobacco industry that are the subject of this viewpoint?

2. The article quotes Cheryl Healton, who is a critic of the tobacco industry ads. Who does Cheryl Healton represent?

3. According to Cheryl Healton, who produces the most effective ads aimed at preventing youth smoking?

A new study. . .proves that youth smoking prevention ads created by the tobacco industry [and] aimed at parents, actually increase the likelihood that teens will smoke in the future. The study, "Impact of Televised Tobacco Industry Smoking Prevention Advertising on Youth Smoking-Related Beliefs, Intentions and Behavior," [was recently published in] the *American Journal of Public Health*.

A Hard Look at Tobacco Prevention Ads

The study is the first to examine the specific effects of tobacco company parent-focused advertising on youth. It does, however, support previous findings by the American Legacy Foundation® that ads created by the tobacco industry—ads which the industry claims are aimed at preventing youth from smoking—actually provide no benefit to youth. In fact, the ads that are created for parental audiences but are clearly also seen by teens, are associated with stronger intentions by teens to smoke in the future.

The American Legacy Foundation®, a national public health organization dedicated to building a world where young people reject tobacco and anyone can quit, previously conducted research evaluating tobacco industry smoking prevention ads in its 2002 release of "Getting to the Truth: Assessing Youths' Reactions to the Truth®; and 'Think. Don't Smoke' Tobacco Counter-Marketing Campaigns." That study found that youth had more favorable reactions to the Foundation's truth® youth smoking prevention campaign than Philip Morris' "Think. Don't Smoke" campaign.

"The tobacco industry ads are a trick on young people," said Foundation President and CEO, Cheryl Healton [who holds a doctorate in public health]. "By creating these ads, the industry claims to be trying to help our nation's youth and acts as if these ads are truly aimed at discouraging smoking. However, this study, along with previous research proves that this is simply not the case. The tobacco industry is in the business of selling cigarettes. What does help discourage youth smoking rates are ads and messages provided by sources that are independent of the tobacco industry, like those produced by the public health and tobacco control communities. If the industry really wanted to help curb youth smoking, tobacco executives would pull these ads off the air."

Industry's Ads Can't Be Trusted

In August 2006, Judge Gladys Kessier of the U.S. District Court for the District of Columbia handed down an historic decision finding that the major tobacco companies have defrauded the American public over a period of five decades. Among their deceptive practices, they intentionally marketed to young people in order to recruit "replacement smokers" and then denied conducting such marketing efforts.

"It is clear that the tobacco companies have lied about their marketing practices, and the 'prevention' ads are simply more of the same. This is a clear cut example of 'The fox guarding the hen house,'" said Healton.

Youth and Tobacco Use: Current Estimates

Cigarette Smoking

- Twenty-three percent of high school students in the United States are current cigarette smokers—23% of females and 22.9% of males.

- Eight percent of middle school students in this country are current cigarette smokers, with estimates slightly higher for females (9%) than males (8%).

- Each day in the United States, approximately 4,000 young people between the ages of 12 and 17 years initiate cigarette smoking, and an estimated 1,140 young people become daily cigarette smokers.

Other Tobacco Use

- Thirteen percent of high school students are current cigar smokers, with estimates higher for males (18%) than for females (8%). Nationally, an estimated 5% of all middle school students are current cigar smokers, with estimates of 7% for males and 4% for females.

- An estimated 10% of males in high school are current smokeless tobacco users, as are an estimated 4% of males in middle school.

"Fact Sheet: Youth and Tobacco Use: Current Estimates,"
Centers for Disease Control and Prevention, 2006. www.cdc.gov.

Philip Morris [appeared recently] in front of the U.S. Supreme Court. . .in a case that originated in Oregon, involving punitive damages for a family who lost a loved one to lung cancer.

"The Philip Morris v. Williams case. . .is just another example of the ongoing litigation that is brought against the tobacco industry for its repeated deception," said Healton. "These cases remind us of the very real damage that these products do. If used as directed, cigarettes kill one-third of the people who smoke them."

Alternative Prevention Programs Make Sense

Healton pointed instead to the American Legacy Foundation's truth® youth smoking prevention campaign as an effective way to keep teens from smoking. In 2005, the foundation announced that truth® accelerated the decline in youth smoking rates between 2000 and 2002. Twenty-two percent of the overall decline in youth smoking during these years is attributable directly to the truth®. About 80 percent of smokers begin using tobacco before the age of 18 and one-third of smokers begin before the age of 14.

"A sublime aesthetic pleasure is one that we take in the presence of awe or fear. . . .Many of the sublime pleasures of smoking can be seen in the movies."

Smoking Behavior Should Not Be Censored in the Movies

Evan R. Goldstein

In the following viewpoint, Evan R. Goldstein criticizes the Motion Picture Association of America for a recent decision to take depictions of smoking into account when assigning ratings to movies. The dangers of smoking are widely known, yet 20 percent of the adult population continues to smoke. Goldstein says that smoking is pleasurable and has value to those who do it, and he argues that efforts to suppress images of smoking are the result of a puritanical opposition to beauty and pleasure that has impoverished our culture. Evan R. Goldstein is a staff editor for the Chronicle of Higher Education.

As you read, consider the following questions:

1. What recent action by the Motion Picture Association of America (MPAA) constitutes censorship, according to Richard Klein, author of *Cigarettes Are Sublime*?

2. Is smoking an ordinary pleasure or a sublime pleasure? What does this mean?

3. Why does the author of this viewpoint think the MPAA's censorship of smoking will backfire?

Has there been a worse time to be a smoker? In an ever-expanding swath of the West[ern world], cigarettes are denounced as evil, and smokers are being shamed—and legislated—to the margins of society. Even China, where around two-thirds of men smoke, is reportedly taking steps to curb smoking in some public places. And now this: The Motion Picture Association of America recently announced that "depictions that glamorize smoking or movies that feature pervasive smoking outside of a historic or other mitigating context" will be taken into account by the organization's rating board—joining the ranks of other film taboos such as profanity, nudity, drug use, and violence.

Prudery on the Rise

In all of this, Richard Klein sees a rising tide of American prudery and censorship. "Why not ban overeating on film, or overdrinking on film?" he asks. "If you can ban the representation of one reality—which is that a lot of cool people smoke—then why not just keep going?" Klein is the author of *Cigarettes Are Sublime* which he describes as "a piece of literary criticism, an analysis of popular culture, a political harangue, a theoretical exercise, and an ode to cigarettes." In a recent interview, Klein spoke about what our culture stands to lose if (when?) the last smoldering butt is stamped out. . . .

Despite the fact that for 40 years all the principal institutions in our society have been telling people from a very early age about the dangers of smoking, cigarettes are as alluring and as evocative as they have ever been before. They continue to be immensely attractive to at least 20 percent of the adult population. Every day billions of people around the world are lighting up. Why?

Airbrushing History

Jean-Paul Sartre smoked two packs of cigarettes and several pipefuls of tobacco a day. But for a poster marking the 100th anniversary of Sartre's birth, the French National Library airbrushed a cigarette out of his photograph to avoid violating laws against advertising tobacco.

"Brickbats," July, 2005. www.reason.org.

A Seductive Pleasure

Cigarettes would not be so popular if they did not provide a great many pleasures and a great many benefits. After all, cigarettes taste bad. But it is the bad taste that you quickly learn to love. How is that possible? In *The Critique of Judgment*, [philosopher Immanuel] Kant distinguished sublime aesthetic pleasure from ordinary aesthetic pleasure, like that we might take from a beautiful form. A sublime aesthetic pleasure is one that we take in the presence of awe or fear. These moments are ecstatic precisely because they contain a warning, a reminder of our own mortality. In other words, the pleasure is found in the poison. It is not in spite of its harmfulness, but rather because it is a harmful substance that people derive so much pleasure from smoking. That is what Kant very technically and specifically calls sublime aesthetic pleasure.

Many of the sublime pleasures of smoking can be seen in the movies. For instance, in *My Best Friend's Wedding* when Julia Roberts hunkers down in moments of the greatest loss and desperation, she is smoking furiously. The cigarette is a friend and a form of consolation. Smoking is a remarkable tool for mitigating anxiety. And it also happens to be beautiful. Movies attest wonderfully to the Promethean beauty of fire, smoke, and ash that cigarettes evoke.

Censoring Beauty

The MPAA decision to take into account depictions of smoking when rating films is a form of censorship. It is a discouraging but unsurprising development. America has always been a Puritan country that harbors a deep resentment against pleasure. But this puritanical opposition to beauty impoverishes our culture. There is a long paragraph at the end of *Being and Nothingness* in which [French philosopher] Jean-Paul Sartre explains how cigarettes allowed him to appropriate the world. And by that he meant that every time he found himself in a new situation—before a beautiful landscape or in the theater or reading a book—whenever he had a momentous moment to celebrate or consecrate, he would light a cigarette. And in so doing, it somehow turns the moment into an idea. Cigarettes allowed him to experience life. And he even says that life without cigarettes is not worth living.

If advocates of this new ratings system think that adolescents are going to be deceived because the motion picture industry censors the seductive charms of smoking, I think they are disastrously mistaken. Censorship inevitably incites the very practice it wishes to inhibit. The more disreputable cigarettes become, the more the taboo provokes interest, arouses fascination, and becomes dangerously compulsive.

In a certain sense, those who continue to light up are offering a brazen protest on behalf of freedom for all of us. Public health used to be about typhoid and drinking water. Now the role of public health has become to warn us against our own bad habits, and to more and more inhibit our pleasures: how we eat, smoke, drink, and all the rest. It is a very intimate, very menacing form of social control.

> *"Despite years of effort by anti-tobacco forces to curb cigarette marketing and advertising aimed at young people, alluring images of smoking are still pervasive in the entertainment media."*

Images of Smoking in the Media Encourage Youth to Smoke

Tara Parker-Pope

In the following viewpoint, Tara Parker-Pope argues that images of smoking have become pervasive in the media, with an average of 12.8 smoking incidents per hour in the top-grossing films of 2004 and 2005. This has occurred even as actual rates of smoking among adults have decreased. Children who are exposed to pro-tobacco images are more likely to start smoking, she says, and claims that parents, and society in general, should understand the impact of these images and limit their children's exposure to pro-smoking messages. Tara Parker-Pope writes for the Wall Street Journal.

Tara Parker-Pope, "Images Continue to Entice Kids to Smoke," *Wall Street Journal*, May 16, 2007. Reprinted with permission of *The Wall Street Journal*, conveyed through Copyright Clearance Center, Inc.

As you read, consider the following questions:

1. What percent of top-grossing movies depict smoking, according to the American Lung Association?
2. What is the percentage of adults and high school students who actually smoke?
3. What decision did model Tyra Banks make about smoking on her television show "America's Next Top Model"?

On a recent episode of the hit TV show "America's Next Top Model," the model hopefuls were shown lounging by the pool and puffing away on cigarettes.

It was a jarring image, particularly for a show that has an unusually high viewership of preteen and adolescent girls. Several studies show that regular exposure to smoking images on television and in movies dramatically increases a child's risk for trying cigarettes and becoming a smoker.

Images of Smoking Are Everywhere

Despite years of effort by anti-tobacco forces to curb cigarette marketing and advertising aimed at young people, alluring images of smoking are still pervasive in the entertainment media.

Of the 50 top-grossing films of 2004 and 2005, 66 percent contained depictions of smoking, with an average frequency of 12.8 incidents per hour, according to research by the American Lung Association chapter in Sacramento. That's the highest measured incidence in a decade. Notably, the incidence of smoking in the movies is far higher than in real life, where about 21 percent of U.S. adults and about 22 percent of high school students smoke, according to the Centers for Disease Control and Prevention.

The issue of smoking in the media was in the spotlight [recently] when the Motion Picture Association of America [MPAA] said it would consider smoking images as a factor in determining movie ratings, along with sex, violence and drug

Smoking in the Movies

Tobacco companies have taken advantage of the powerful influence movies have on people's behavior to popularize and normalize smoking.

Despite legally binding pledges from tobacco companies to stop paying cash for brand placement, tobacco brands still appear in movies.

Portrayals of smoking in movies promote the same themes as other tobacco advertising: rebellion, independence, sexiness, wealth, power and celebration.

Rarely do movies depict the realities of smoking—characters suffering from smoke related diseases and the effects of secondhand smoke.

Scientific research confirms that on-screen smoking strongly influences young people to start smoking.

Seventy-five percent of PG-13 rated movies and 40% of movies rated G and PG contain tobacco images.

Expose Big Tobacco. www.exposebigtobacco.com.

use. The decision falls far short of what tobacco control groups want: a mandatory R rating for any movie with smoking in it.

"While smoking has come down among adults, it's actually going up in the movies and that is worrisome," said Barry R. Bloom, dean of the Harvard School of Public Health, which made a presentation to the MPAA about the impact of smoking in the movies.

Looking Up to Celebrities

The data are compelling. [In 2006] researchers at the University of Massachusetts Medical School in Worcester reviewed more than 50 studies looking at kids' exposure to tobacco marketing and media images. They found that children who were regularly exposed to pro-tobacco images such as movie images where an appealing lead character smokes were twice as likely to start smoking as children with lower media exposure, according to the study published in the *Archives of Pediatrics and Adolescent Medicine.*

"If the average kid sees an actor in whom he or she is not interested, smoking has some impact," said Robert J. Wellman, professor of behavioral sciences at Fitchburg State College in Fitchburg, Mass., and lead author of the review article. "But if he or she sees a favorite actor smoking, it has much more of an impact."

But while the movie group's decision fell short of a mandatory R rating for smoking scenes, tobacco-control experts say there are things that parents can do to lower kids' risk for smoking.

Experts say parents should limit kids' exposure to R-rated movies. The lung association research showed that R-rated films averaged 20.4 smoking images per hour, compared with 14.2 in PG-13 films. A recent study of kids in New Zealand showed that the more R-rated movies kids watch, the more likely they are to smoke or be heavier smokers, Bloom said.

Reducing kids' overall media exposure and taking TV out of the kids' bedroom may also help. Researchers at the University of North Carolina at Chapel Hill recently showed that kids who have a television in the bedroom are more likely to try smoking than kids without bedroom TVs, according to the study published [recently] in the *Archives of Pediatrics and Adolescent Medicine.* With a TV in their room, not only are kids about twice as likely to watch R-rated movies, but also parents aren't nearby to remind them about the perils of smoking when they see an image on television.

"Isolated Viewing" Is a Factor

"Kids who have bedroom TVs have more isolated viewing time," said study lead author Christine Jackson, a senior research scientist at RTI International in Research Triangle Park

[North Carolina], an independent research organization that focuses on social problems. "Kids who have TVs in the bedroom aren't getting the counter-arguing from parents."

At "America's Next Top Model," the show's executive producers Ken Mok and Tyra Banks noticed that this season's crop of contestants were unusually heavy smokers. As a result, they decided that next season, the house where the contestants live is going to be smoke-free, and one of the featured photo shoots will have a strong anti-smoking message.

"Tyra and I understand the influence 'Top Model' has on a generation of young people, and we want to make sure we get the right message to our audience," Mok said.

Periodical Bibliography

The following articles have been selected to supplement the diverse views in this chapter.

Brooks Boliek — "Pol to H'wood: Do More to Clear Air," *Hollywood Reporter*, June 25, 2007.

Thomas Briant — "Changing Opinions: NATO Joins with Heartland Institute to Create Education Campaign Aimed at Dubious Anti-Tobacco Claims," *National Petroleum News*, December 2006.

Harvard Reviews of Health News — "Kids May Imitate Movie Smoking," 2007.

Bradley Johnson — "Marlboro Man Rides into the Sunset," *Advertising Age*, June 25, 2007.

Jeffrey Kluger — "Hollywood's Smoke Alarm," *Time International*, April 30, 2007.

Mark R. Madler — "Tobacco Industry Wants to Snuff Out Role in Films: Cigarette Makers Make Appeal in Trade Ads," *San Fernando Valley Business Journal*, December 4, 2006.

New Mexico Business Journal — "New Report: Tobacco Companies Spend Massive $48.0 Million a Year on Marketing in New Mexico," August 2007.

Betsy Spethmann — "Tobacco Marketing Drops to $13 Billion: Advocates Call for Regulation," *Promo*, April 30, 2007.

Andrew Tyndall — "Too Much Smoke, Too Little Coverage: Though the Industry Was Stunned to Learn of Peter Jennings' Lung Cancer, in Recent Years Network News Has Turned Down the Heat on the Health Dangers of Tobacco," *Broadcasting & Cable*, April 11, 2005.

USA Today — "Up in Smoke," October 2006.

For Further Discussion

Chapter 1

1. According to the National Institute of Drug Abuse, most smokers use tobacco because they are addicted to nicotine. According to Paul Johnson, on the other hand, smoking helps his friends to sleep better, and reduces feelings of melancholia or sadness. Which viewpoint do you think is right?

2. Paul Johnson says that the war on tobacco "makes little sense" because while tobacco users may be hurting themselves, they are not causing harm or injury to other people. Richard Carmona, former U.S. Surgeon General, disagrees with this opinion, claiming that exposure to secondhand smoke endangers the health of non-smokers. What do you think?

Chapter 2

1. Studies have shown that increasing taxes on tobacco leads to significant reduction in smoking behavior, and Prabhat Jha suggests that this is reason enough to impose heavy taxes on cigarettes. A.O. Kime argues that this places an unfair burden on smokers, especially since many states do not use cigarette revenues to address the health effects of smoking. Do you think it is right for states to tax cigarettes in order to encourage people to quit smoking? If so, how do you think cigarette revenues should be used? Should states be able to use cigarette revenues to fund education, pay for road maintenance, or make improvements to public parks? Or should cigarette tax revenues be dedicated to smoking-related health initiatives?

2. Most Americans now believe that smoking should be banned in public places, Stephen Kaufman asserts. For this reason, more and more localities are passing laws banning smoking. However, A. O. Kime believes that restrictions on public smoking violate individual rights. In deciding whether smoking should be banned, should localities place more weight on public opinion, or on the rights of individuals?

Chapter 3

1. Andrew C. von Eschenbach, Commissioner of Food and Drugs for the U.S. Food and Drug Administration (FDA), feels it is inappropriate for the FDA to regulate tobacco, because of the known health dangers. Do you agree with him that regulation of tobacco by the FDA would send the message that smoking and tobacco use are safe?

2. Senator Edward Kennedy and Andrew C. von Eschenbach differ in their understanding of the role of the FDA. Compare and contrast those understandings.

3. How do you think Joseph A. Rotondi would describe the mission of the FDA? Do you think he is right in believing that tobacco manufacturers benefit from regulation, and also benefit from alliances with some anti-smoking groups? If he is right that the tobacco industry benefits most from regulation, are there any losers?

Chapter 4

1. In the first viewpoint in this chapter, Physicians for a Smoke-Free Canada takes the position that tobacco advertising increases unhealthy behaviors by making statements about tobacco use that are not true. This organization wants to ban tobacco advertising, or, alternatively, to tax tobacco promotions in order to recoup some of the health care costs caused by tobacco use. The advertising industry representatives of the second viewpoint disagree, arguing

that any restrictions on tobacco advertising in the United States would infringe on the First Amendment rights of the tobacco interests. Do you think it is possible to make a judgment about the truthfulness of a particular tobacco promotion? Should governments regulate commercial speech about tobacco to ensure that the content of tobacco advertising is not misleading to consumers?

2. In the third viewpoint in this chapter, Cheryl Healton is quoted by the authors as stating that tobacco industry ads, which claim to reduce smoking behaviors among youth, in fact have the opposite effect, making it more likely that young people will choose to smoke. Do you think tobacco interests should be required to produce advertising aimed at reducing youth smoking? Do you think that such ads can be trusted?

3. In the fourth viewpoint, Evan R. Goldstein talks about "the sublime pleasures of smoking." What does he mean by this?

4. Do you agree with Evan R. Goldstein that taking depictions of smoking into account when rating motion pictures amounts to a form of censorship? Why does it matter if young people do or do not see depictions of smoking in the movies?

Organizations to Contact

The editors have compiled the following list of organizations concerned with the issues debated in this book. The descriptions are derived from materials provided by the organizations. All have publications or information available for interested readers. The list was compiled on the date of publication of the present volume; the information provided here may change. Readers need to remember that many organizations take several weeks or longer to respond to inquiries.

American Cancer Society
901 E St. NW, Suite 500, Washington, DC   20004
(800) ACS-2345
Web site: www.cancer.org

The mission of the American Cancer Society (ACS) is to eliminate cancer as a major health problem through research, education, advocacy, and service. The ACS works collaboratively with national partners to implement comprehensive tobacco control programs. It advocates for social and environmental changes at the national, state, and community levels that prevent young people from starting to use tobacco, and provides support for those who wish to stop smoking. The ACS Web site includes tobacco-related resources on topics such as smoking, tobacco and health, and the international tobacco control movement.

American Council on Science and Health
1995 Broadway, 2nd Floor, New York, NY   10023-5860
(212) 362-7044 • fax: (212) 362-4919
e-mail: acsh@acsh.org
Web site: www.acsh.org

The American Council on Science and Health is a nonprofit consumer education consortium concerned with the scientific basis of public policies related to health and the environment.

It publishes editorials, position papers, and books on a range of health-related issues. Tobacco use is one of nine topics that is specifically addressed on the organization's Web site.

American Lung Association
61 Broadway, 6th Floor, New York, NY   10006
(212) 315-8700
Web site: www.lungusa.org

The American Lung Association (ALA) is a publicly funded nonprofit organization concerned with the causes of lung disease, including tobacco use, and also with the prevention of lung disease. The ALA Web site includes pages on research and treatment of lung disease, as well as a section on tobacco control.

Campaign for Tobacco Free Kids
1400 Eye St., Suite 1200, Washington, DC   20005
(202) 296-5469
Web site: www.tobaccofreekids.org

The Campaign for Tobacco-Free Kids aims to change public attitudes and policies on tobacco by educating the public and policy makers about tobacco, exposing the tobacco industry's efforts to market to children, advocating solutions that reduce tobacco use and exposure to secondhand smoke, and mobilizing organizations and individuals to fight against tobacco use. The organization's Web site includes a series of special reports on issues like smokeless tobacco, tobacco-free schools, and how the consumption of tobacco is influenced by the cost of tobacco products.

Cato Institute
1000 Massachusetts Ave. NW, Washington, DC   20001-5403
(202) 842-0200 • fax: (202) 842-3490
e-mail: cato@cato.org
Web site: www.cato.org

The Cato Institute is a libertarian public policy research foundation dedicated to limiting the role of government and protecting individual rights. It is opposed to most forms of government regulation. The Web site of the Cato Institute includes a variety of editorials and policy papers addressing the tobacco industry and the regulatory environment.

Competitive Enterprise Institute
1001 Connecticut Ave. NW, Washington, DC   20036
(202) 331-1010 • fax: (202) 331-0640
Web site: http://cei.org

The Competitive Enterprise Institute (CEI) is a nonprofit public policy organization dedicated to advancing the principles of free enterprise and limited government. It believes that individuals are best helped not by government intervention, but by making their own choices in a free marketplace. CEI opposes any government role in the regulation of tobacco products and supports the principle of individual choice. A search engine on the site provides access to articles and opinion pieces, mostly addressing the issue of government regulation of tobacco products.

Heartland Institute
19 South LaSalle St., Suite 903, Chicago, IL   60603
(312) 377-4000
e-mail: think@heartland.org
Web site: www.heartland.org

The mission of the Heartland Institute is to discover, develop, and promote free-market solutions to social and economic problems. Such solutions include choice and personal responsibility in health care, market-based approaches to environmental protection, privatization of public services, and deregulation in areas it believes are better controlled by property rights and markets. The Heartland Institute Web site includes a number of documents concerning state taxation of tobacco, federal regulation of tobacco products, and the harm-reduction concept.

National Center on Addiction and Substance Abuse at Columbia University

633 Third Ave., 19th Floor, New York, NY   10017-6706
(212) 841-5200
Web site: www.casacolumbia.org

Founded in 1992 by former U.S. Secretary of Health, Education, and Welfare Joseph A. Califano Jr., the mission the National Center on Addiction and Substance Abuse at Columbia University (CASA) is to inform Americans of the economic and social costs of substance abuse and its impact on their lives, as well as remove the stigma of substance abuse. CASA, whose staff is drawn from medical, social science, and legal fields, studies and combats abuse of all substances—alcohol and nicotine as well as illegal, prescription, and performance enhancing drugs—in all sectors of society.

National Institute on Drug Abuse

6001 Executive Blvd., Bethesda, Maryland   20892
Web site: www.nida.nih.gov

The National Institute on Drug Abuse (NIDA) is part of the National Institutes of Health. NIDA's mission is to use science to combat drug abuse and addiction. It supports and conducts research across a broad range of scientific disciplines and disseminates the results to improve prevention, treatment, and public policy as it relates to drug addiction, including tobacco addiction. The NIDA Web site includes materials on nicotine addiction for students and young adults.

Office of the Surgeon General

5600 Fishers Lane, Room 18-66, Rockville, MD   20857
(301) 443-4000
Web site: www.surgeongeneral.gov

The Surgeon General serves as the United States' chief health educator by providing the best current scientific information available on how to improve health and reduce the risk of illness and injury. The Web site of the Surgeon General's office includes a number of resources addressing tobacco use reduction, including resources on women, smoking, and cancer; the effects of involuntary exposure to tobacco smoke; the Federal Cigarette and Labeling Act; and materials on how to quit smoking.

Philip Morris USA
Consumer Response Center, Richmond, VA   23261
(800) 343-0975
Web site: www.philipmorrisusa.com

Philip Morris USA, a part of Altria Group, Inc., is the leading cigarette manufacturer in the United States. The Philip Morris USA Web site includes extensive resources on smoking and health issues, legislation and regulation, and product information.

U.S. Food and Drug Administration
5600 Fishers Lane, Rockville, MD   20857-0001
(888) 463-6332
Web site: www.fda.gov

The U.S. Food and Drug Administration (FDA) is responsible for protecting the public health by ensuring the safety, efficacy, and security of human and veterinary drugs, biological products, medical devices, the nation's food supply, cosmetics, and products that emit radiation. The FDA also is responsible for advancing the public health by helping to speed innovations that make medicines and foods more effective, safer, and affordable, and by disseminating accurate, science-based medical and nutritional information. The FDA Web site does not contain materials about tobacco products, because the U.S. Supreme Court ruled in 2001 that the agency does not have the authority to regulate tobacco. The FDA Web site does provide a link to www.smokefree.gov, which provides information on how to quit smoking.

Bibliography of Books

William Everett Bailey   *The Invisible Drug.* Houston: Mosaic Publications, 1996.

Allan M. Brandt   *The Cigarette Century: The Rise, Fall and Deadly Persistence of the Product That Defined America.* New York: Basic Books, 2007.

Eric Burns   *The Smoke of the Gods: A Social History of Tobacco.* Philadelphia: Temple University Press, 2007.

Congressional Information Service   *FDA Regulaton of Tobacco Products: A Policy and Legal Analysis.* Washington, DC: Library of Congress, 2004.

David T. Courtwright   *Forces of Habit: Drugs and the Making of the Modern World.* Cambridge, MA: Harvard University Press, 2002.

D. Kirk Davidson   *Selling Sin: The Marketing of Socially Unacceptable Products.* Westport, CT: Praeger, 2003.

Iain Gately   *Tobacco: The Story of How Tobacco Seduced the World.* New York: Grove Press, 2001.

Sander L. Gilman and Zhou Xun   *Smoke: A Global History of Smoking.* London: Reaktion Books, 2004.

Gio B. Gori   *Virtually Safe Cigarettes: Reviving an Opportunity Once Tragically Rejected.* Amsterdam: IOS Press, 2000.

K.O. Haustein — *Tobacco or Health: Physiological and Social Damages Caused by Tobacco Smoking.* New York: Springer, 2003.

Eileen Heyes — *Tobacco USA: The Industry Behind the Smoke Curtain.* Brookfield, CT: Millbrook Press, 1999.

Peter D. Jacobson — *Combating Teen Smoking: Research and Policy Strategies.* Ann Arbor: University of Michigan Press, 2001.

David A. Kessler — *A Question of Intent: A Great American Battle with a Deadly Industry.* New York: PublicAffairs, 2001.

Susan Linn — *Consuming Kids: The Hostile Takeover of Childhood.* New York: New Press, 2004.

Barbara S. Lynch and Richard J. Bonnie — *Growing Up Tobacco Free: Preventing Nicotine Addiction in Children and Youths.* Washington, DC: National Academy Press, 1994.

Tara Parker-Pope — *Cigarettes: Anatomy of an Industry from Seed to Smoke.* New York: New Press, 2001.

Oakley Stern Ray and Charles Ksir — *Drugs, Society and Human Behavior.* Boston: McGraw-Hill, 2004.

Clete Snell — *Peddling Poison: The Tobacco Industry and Kids.* Westport, CT: Praeger, 2005.

Lesley Stern — *The Smoking Book.* Chicago: University of Chicago Press, 1999.

U.S. Department of Health and Human Services
Preventing Tobacco Use Among Young People: A Report of the Surgeon General. Washington, DC: Centers for Disease Control and Prevention, 1994.

William J. Vizzard
In the Cross Fire: A Political History of the Bureau of Alcohol, Tobacco and Firearms. Boulder, CO: Lynne Rienner Publishers, 1997.

William C. Winter
Tobacco Use by Native North Americans: Sacred Smoke and Silent Killer. Norman: University of Oklahoma Press, 2000.

Index

A

ACS. *See* American Cancer Society
Action on Smoking and Health (ASH), 91–92
Addictive effect, nicotine, 26–28
Advertising/marketing
  cigarette bans, 177–188
  costs of, 167, 169–170
  current ads, 166–167
  deception, 143, 194
  decreasing benefit, 170–172
  doesn't cause smoking, 176–186
  ever-safer cigarettes, 157
  FDA regulation, 21, 120–122, 144–145
  government measures, 173–174
  health warnings, 21
  Joe Camel campaign, 91, 107, 176, 180–183, 185–186
  legal guidelines, 114–115, 169, 181
  limitations/restrictions on, 14–15, 77, 109, 161
  media bans, 146
  prevention programs, 120–121, 143, 169, 187–191
  profit increases, 164–165
  public-policy effect on, 168–169
  ratifying FCTC, 174–175
  research impact on, 183–186
  to youth/children, 75, 121–122, 162, 187–191, 196–200
The Affluent Society (Galbraith), 178
Air contamination, 29, 87, 92

ALA. *See* American Lung Association
Alcohol use, 69, 71, 88, 102
Altadis U.S.A. Inc. v. Reilly, 162
Altria Group, 136–137
American Cancer Society (ACS), 16–17, 21, 105, 178
American Council on Science and Health (ACSH), 56–58
American Heart Association, 16–17, 114–115
American Legacy Foundation, 15, 65, 187–191
American Lung Association (ALA), 16–17, 197
Americans for Nonsmokers' Rights, 91
America's Next Top Model (TV show), 197, 200
Anti-smoking lobbyists
  advertising campaigns, 97, 145, 150, 180
  antitrust laws, 16
  litigation concerns, 137
  media bans, 56, 100, 145, 200
  nonsmoker protection by, 91, 96, 98
  See also Nonsmokers
Archives of Pediatrics and Adolescent Medicine (AMA), 199
Asthma symptom aggravation, 28–29, 40, 104

B

Banning smoking. *See* Smoking bans
Banzhaf, John F., 92–94
Bast, Joseph, 95–100

Bayer, Ronald, 106–111

Being and Nothingness (Sartre), 195

Bernstein, Henry H., 101–105

Black-market cigarettes, 85–86, 156

Bloom, Barry R., 198

Boddewyn, Jean J., 185

Bonnie, Richard, 98

Bootlegger-Baptist coalitions, 142–148

British American Tobacco (BAT), 58–59

British Medical Journal (journal), 99

A Broken Promise to Our Children: The 1998 State Tobacco Settlement Nine Years Later (ALA), 17

Bronchitis, 21, 28, 144

Buckley, William F., 80

Bull Durham smoking tobacco, 180

Bush, George W., 68, 70, 133

Business Wire, 49–53

C

California
ACS data, 99
advertising statistics, 183
Air Resources Board, 92
tobacco-control program, 74–75

Campaign for Tobacco-Free Kids, 16–17, 139–140

Cancer
death rates, 74–75
nicotine link, 58
NNK agent, 53
nonsmoker deaths, 28–29
risk of, 83
secondhand smoke, 36, 38–39, 45–47, 92, 99
smokeless tobacco, 50–53
smoking-related, 15, 21–22, 28–29, 55
surgeon general report, 144
tobacco cause, 128
tobacco-tax impact, 83

Carcinogenesis threshold, 39

Carcinogens/carcinogenic environments
child exposure to, 37
disclosure of, 114–115
secondhand smoke in, 45, 98
in tobacco, 128

Carlyle, Thomas, 32–34

Carmona, Richard, 36–43, 45–46

Catholic priests, 32, 35

Cato Institute, 15–16

Celebrity smoking, impact on youth, 198–199

Centers for Disease Control and Prevention (CDC), 17
child smoking suggestions, 103–104
cotinine levels, 100
Office on Smoking and Health, 21
smokeless tobacco, 50–51, 53
smoking research, 197
smoking statistics, 55, 63–64
tobacco control, defined, 74

Cessation programs
FDA access, 134
funding for, 15, 17, 61, 64
health benefits of, 54–56, 77
non-nicotine programs, 129
participation in, 110, 140
tobacco taxes, 77–78
withdrawal symptoms peak during, 27
See also Prevention programs

Children and smoking
    advertising/marketing, 64, 121–122, 162, 187–191, 196–200
    asthma increase, 28–29
    carcinogenic environments, 37
    cigarette taxes, 109
    cost increases, 79
    Five D's to quit, 104
    prevention efforts/goals, 77, 101–111, 118, 179–180
    secondhand smoke, 37, 40–43, 47, 105
    smokeless tobacco, 52, 162
    suggestions to parents, 102–104
    See also Teen smoking
China, smoking-related deaths, 77–78
Cigarettes
    advertising bans, 21, 177–188
    black market, 85–86, 156
    ever-safer, 157
    filtered, 21, 86
    low-tar, 21, 99, 143, 145, 148
    price increases, 16, 65, 79
    smuggling, 78–79, 133
    taxes on, 109
    warning labels on, 21, 59, 123–124
    See also Nicotine; Smoking/ smokers; Tobacco use
Cigarettes Are Sublime (Klein), 193
Clinton, Bill, 107, 182
Coalition on Smoking or Health, 181–182
Cole, Phillip, 56
Constable, Burt, 40
Cornyn, John, 115
Corr, William V., 61–66

Cotinine (nicotine metabolite), 41–42, 100, 105
The Critique of Judgment (Kant), 194

D

Davis, Tom, 115
Deceptive advertising, 143, 194
Drinking vs. smoking, 23, 28, 31–32, 35
Drugs/drug use
    FDA regulation, 128–129, 132–133
    nicotine as, 151
    nicotine-replacement systems, 58, 127
    in smokers, 102
    in teenagers, 67–71
    tobacco as, 23, 25–27, 114, 124
    war on, 81–82, 85
Durning, Alan Thein, 179

E

Ecstasy (recreational drug), 68, 70
Emphysema, 15, 28, 58, 145
Ending the Tobacco Problem (Bonnie), 98
Eschenbach, Andrew C. von, 126–134, 142, 148
Ever-safer cigarette, 157

F

Family Smoking Prevention and Tobacco Control Act, 52, 115–116, 130
FCTC. *See* Framework Convention on Tobacco Control
FDA. *See* Food and Drug Administration

Federal Cigarette Labeling and Advertising Act, 21

Federal Communication Commission (FCC), 145

Federal Trade Commission (FTC), 53, 143–145, 182

Filtered cigarettes, 21, 86

Final Rule by FDA, 109

First Amendment rights, 3, 114, 121, 161–162

Fischer, Paul M., 182

Five D's to quit smoking, 104

Food and Drug Administration (FDA), regulation/legislation

    advertising concerns, 21, 120–122, 144–145

    drugs/drug use, 128–129, 132–133

    is misguided, 149–158

    litigation protection, 135–140

    new product lines, 50–51

    nicotine-replacement products, 129

    restricts marketing, 64

    rulings, 109, 114

    should be allowed, 117–125

    should not be allowed, 126–134

    tobacco company benefit, 141–148

Forces International, 149–158

Framework Convention on Tobacco Control (FCTC), 42, 174–175

Franklin, Benjamin, 80

G

Galbraith, John Kenneth, 178–179

Gates Foundation, 80

Gershman, Dave, 67–71

"Getting to the Truth: Assessing Youths' Reactions to the Truth" (research study), 189

Global tobacco control treaty (WHO), 80

Godshall, William T., 16, 54–60

Goldstein, Evan R., 192–195

Gonzaga, Ignatius, 32

Goodin, Robert, 108

Goodman, Jordan, 180

Great American Smokeout, 102

Grey, Simon, 32

H

Hayek, Friedrich, 100

Health Affairs (journal), 17

The Health Consequences of Involuntary Smoking (Surgeon General report), 38, 42–43, 128

Health impact of smoking

    from advertising, 21, 163–175

    air contamination, 29, 87, 92

    alcohol use, 69, 71, 88, 102

    asthma symptom aggravation, 28–29, 40, 104

    black-market cigarettes, 85–86

    bronchitis, 21, 28, 144

    dangers exaggerated, 30–35

    emphysema, 15, 28, 58, 145

    FDA regulation/legislation, 118–119, 125, 130–134

    harmful effects, 23–29

    health-care costs, 87, 97

    heart disease/damage, 15, 22, 29, 45–46, 74, 99, 128

    mentally ill smokers, 24–25

    misleading information, 124

    MSA settlement, 15–18

    SIDS incidence, 29, 104–105, 128

    TIRC tests, 21

tobacco company claims, 139–140, 142

tobacco costs on, 65–66

tobacco taxes and, 77–78, 82–83

See also Cancer; Children and smoking; Drugs/drug use; Nicotine; Secondhand smoke; Smokeless tobacco; Teen smoking; Tobacco use

Healthy People 2010 initiative, 43

Healton, Cheryl, 189, 191

Heart disease/damage, 15, 22, 29, 45–46, 74, 99, 128

Heartland Institute, 96, 100

The Hidden Persuaders (Packard), 178

Hitt, Dave, 47

Hockney, David, 32

I

Impact of Televised Tobacco Industry Smoking Prevention Advertising on Youth Smoking-Related Beliefs, Intentions and Behavior (research study), 188

India, smoking-related deaths, 77

Insecticide sprays, nicotine levels, 29

Institute of Medicine (IOM)
    advertising impact, 121
    FDA authority, 119, 151
    legislative actions, 64
    prevention stance, 108
    safer cigarettes, 150–151

J

Jackson, Christine, 200

Jacobson, Jed, 50

Jesuit smoking, 32

Jha, Prabhat, 76–80

Joe Camel advertising campaign, 91, 107, 176, 180–183, 185–186

John Hopkins University, 21

Johnson, Paul, 30–35

Johnston, Lloyd, 68–69

Journal of the American Medical Association, 180, 182

Junk-science argument, 97–99

K

Kant, Immanuel, 194

Kaufman Stephen, 90–94

Kennedy, Edward M., 115, 117–125

Kentucky excise tax, 60

Kessier, Gladys, 189

Kessler, David, 107, 146, 178–179

Kiesig, Valeri, 106–111

Kime, A. O., 81–89

Klein, Richard, 193

Knox, Father Ronald, 32

Koop, C. Everett, 38, 43

Kozlowski, Lynn, 56

L

Lamb, Charles, 32

Lancet (British medical journal), 56

Lee, Christopher, 122

Legal claims/legality, of smoking/tobacco
    for advertising, 114–115, 169, 181
    cigarettes to children, 122
    FDA guidelines, 114, 118, 132, 150
    MSA implementation, 15
    outdoor smoke, 92
    settlements, 64–65, 85, 91, 170
    smokeless tobacco, 52

against tobacco companies, 84, 137, 172, 198
See also Tobacco Master Settlement Agreement
Legislation. *See* Food and Drug Administration
Lesperance, Leann M., 101–105
Liggett Tobacco Company, 146
Lombardi Comprehensive Cancer Center, 57
Lorillard Tobacco Company v. Reilly, 162
Low-tar cigarettes, 21, 99, 143, 145, 148
Lung cancer. *See* Cancer

M

Margaret (Princess of England), 34–35
Margolis, Liz, 71
Marijuana (recreational drug), 47, 71, 88
Marketing. *See* Advertising/ marketing
McGovern, Janet Audrain, 110
McGowan, Joan, 50–52
Media impact on smoking
    doesn't cause smoking, 176– 186
    encouraging youth, 187–191, 196–200
    harm to public health, 163– 175
    movie censorship, 192–195
    prevention ads, 187–191
    statistical significance, 183– 186
Medical consequences. *See* Health impact of smoking
Melly, George, 32
Mentally ill smokers, 24–25
Mill, John Stuart, 11, 96

Milloy, Courtland, 180
Model Statute, 15
Mok, Ken, 200
Monitoring the Future Survey (NIDA report), 24, 62–64, 68
    pulmonary disease, 28
Motion Picture Association of America (MPAA), 193–195, 197– 198
Movies, smoking depiction, 143, 192–195, 197–199
Mr. Sponge's Sporting Tour (Surtees), 34
My Best Friend's Wedding (movie), 194

N

Nasal snuff (tobacco), 20, 25, 50, 52–53, 56
National Cancer Institute (NCI), 53, 152
National Clearinghouse for Smoking and Health, 21
National Institute on Drug Abuse (NIDA), 23–29, 62–64
National Survey on Drug Use and Health, 24
NGOs. *See* Nongovernmental agencies (NGOs)
Nicotine
    addictive effect, 26–28
    cancer link, 58
    cotinine, 41–42, 100, 105
    as drug, 151
    insecticide sprays in, 29
    replacement products, 129
    smokeless tobacco and, 53
    in tobacco smoke, 25–26
    tobacco taxes, 87
    See also Cigarettes; Health impact of smoking; Tobacco use

Nicotine replacement therapy (NRT), 58–59

NIDA. *See* National Institute on Drug Abuse

NNK, cancer-causing agent, 53

Nongovernmental agencies (NGOs), 74

Nonsmokers

cancer in, 28–29

death rates of, 98

labeling benefits, 153

public smoking bans, 90–94, 100

secondhand smoke, 36–43, 98–100, 138

SIDS risks among, 104–105

tax benefits, 97

See also Anti-smoking lobbyists

Novello, Antonia, 181

O

O'Brien, Thomas C., 15–16

Organization for Economic Cooperation and Development (OECD), 78

OxyContin (painkiller), 70

P

Packard, Vance, 178–179

Parker-Pope, Tara, 196–200

Passive smoke. *See* Secondhand smoke

Paternalism vs. individualism, children smoking, 110–111

Philip Morris Company, 91, 136–140

Philip Morris v. Williams, 190–191

Physicians for a Smoke-Free Canada, 163–175

Potentially reduced exposure products (PREPs), 57, 138–139

Predictors of Participation in a Smoking Cessation Program Among Young Adult Smokers (McGovern et al), 110

Premature death epidemic, poor countries, 77

President's Cancer Panel, 64

Preventable cause of death, smoking, 25, 67, 77, 118, 138

Preventing Tobacco Use Among Young People (1994 Surgeon General report), 108

Prevention programs

advertising limits, 120–121, 143, 169, 187–191

alternatives to, 191

for bad behavior, 32–34

through CDC, 50–51, 53, 74

for children/youths, 75, 101–111

MSA funds for, 15, 17

of NGOs, 74

to reduce/prevent smoking, 69–70, 128–130, 170

states' reduction of, 87

for teen smoking, 61–66

tobacco industry ads, 187–191

tobacco revenue for, 84

See also Cessation programs

Price increases, tobacco, 16, 65, 79

Priestly, J. B., 32

Public Health Service, 21

Pulmonary disease, 28

R

R. J. Reynolds Tobacco Company, 180, 182–183

Raleigh, Sir Walter, 31

Regulation. *See* Food and Drug Administration

Residential fire risk, smoking, 29

Rights violations of smokers, 82, 85–89, 96–97

Ritalin (prescription drug), 71

Rodu, Brad, 54–60, 56

Rolfe, John, 14

Rotondi, Joseph A., 141–148

Russell, Michael A. H., 56

S

Sartre, Jean-Paul, 195

Schudson, Michael, 183–184

Secondhand smoke

    attitudes toward, 37–38

    cancer from, 36, 38–39, 45–47, 92, 99

    causal relations, 99

    children, exposure to, 37, 40–43, 47, 105

    cotinine levels, 41–42, 100, 105

    dangers exaggerated, 44–48, 86–87

    exposure reduction, 41–42

    nonsmoker risk, 36–43, 98–100, 138

    smoking bans, 45–46

Sen, Amartya, 80

Senate bill 625. *See* Family Smoking Prevention and Tobacco Control Act

Settlements. *See* Legal claims/legality; Tobacco Master Settlement Agreement

SIDS. *See* Sudden infant death syndrome

Siegel, Michael, 46, 135–140

Smokefree Pennsylvania, 16

Smokeless tobacco

    abuse of, 24–26

    advertising for, 161, 179

    children/youth usage, 161, 190

    effect delivery system, 25

    harmful to health, 49–53

    harms less than smoking, 54–60

    nicotine content in, 53

    snus, 50, 52, 59

    warning labels for, 123

Smokeless Tobacco and How to Quit (ACS), 51

Smoking bans

    advertising concerns, 177–188

    in Calabasis, CA, 92–93

    coercion unnecessary, 99–100

    cost concerns, 97–98

    junk science basis, 98–99

    laws, 91

    in media, 56, 100, 145, 146, 200

    for nonsmokers, 90–94, 100

    in public, favorable, 90–94

    in public, not favorable, 95–100

    secondhand smoke concerns, 45–46

Smoking/smokers

    advertising doesn't cause, 176–186

    danger exaggerated, 30–35, 44–48, 86–87

    vs. drinkers, 23, 28, 31–32, 35

    drug use of, 102

    mentally ill as, 24–25

    movie depiction of, 143, 192

    residential fire risk, 29

    rights violations, 82, 85–89, 95–97

    television as factor, 145, 177, 197, 199–200

    worldwide reduction, 80

    See also Children and smoking; Cigarettes; Health impact of smoking; Legal claims/legality; Media impact on smoking; Second-hand smoke; Teen smoking

Smuggling cigarettes, 78–79, 133

Snuff. *See* Nasal snuff (tobacco)

Snus (smokeless tobacco), 50, 52, 59

Steinfeld, Jesse (Surgeon General), 38

Sudden infant death syndrome (SIDS), 29, 104–105, 128

Sullum, Jacob, 44–48, 176–186

Surtees, Robert Smith, 34

T

Tax on tobacco. *See* Tobacco taxes

Teen smoking
    advertising as factor, 179, 187–191
    cessation efforts, 24, 61–66, 101, 103–104
    FDA programs, 120
    rates declining, 62, 67–71, 94
    reduction efforts stalled, 61–66
    risk factors, 184–185
    smokeless tobacco, 51

Television as smoking factor, 145, 177, 197, 199–200

Tennyson, Alfred Lord, 32–34

Think, Don't Smoke (campaigns), 187, 189

Third National Report on Human Exposure to Environmental Chemicals (CDC), 41–42

Tobacco Industry Research Council (TIRC), 21

Tobacco Master Settlement Agreement (MSA), 14–18, 91, 146–147

Tobacco Product Scientific Advisory Committee, 151

Tobacco taxes
    cancer risk, 83
    cessation programs and, 77–78
    congressional authority, 64
    industry opposition to, 78
    laws unfair, 81–89
    nicotine addiction, 87
    policies, tobacco, 60
    property rights, 86–87
    public-welfare benefit, 80
    rights violation by states, 82, 85
    save lives, 76–80
    settlement funds, 85
    state extortion/tyranny, 84–85, 87–89

Tobacco use
    Bull Durham brand, 180
    California control program, 74075
    campaigns against, 16–17, 139–140
    carcinogens in, 128
    cigarette prices, 65
    control of, 74, 77–78
    delivery system, 25–26
    as drug use, 23, 25–27, 114, 124
    harm reduction, 56–57
    health costs, 65–66
    history of, 20–22, 31
    marketing, 65
    nasal snuff, 20, 25, 50, 52–53, 56
    Native American early use, 20
    as preventable cause of death, 25, 67, 77, 118, 138
    See also Cancer; Cessation programs; Cigarettes; Health impact of smoking; Legal claims/legality; Nicotine; Prevention programs; Smokeless tobacco

U

U.S. Department of Health and Human Services, 43, 129
U.S. Supreme Court
   damage awards by, 136–137
   final rule on nicotine, 122, 190
   Philip Morris case, 190–191
   regulatory jurisdiction, 146
   taxes unconstitutional, 88
   on tobacco advertising, 162
   tobacco labeling, 114–115

V

Victoria (Queen of England), 35
Viscusi, Kip, 97, 99

W

Wall Street Journal (newspaper), 115–116
Warning labels on cigarettes, 21, 59, 123–124
Waxman, Henry A., 115, 122
Wellman, Robert J., 199
Whelan, Elizabeth, 185
World Health Organization (WHO), 57, 74, 79–80, 164

Y

Yandle, Bruce, 142
Youth smoking. *See* Children and smoking